CW00351701

THE POCKET GUIDE TO
TREES
OF
NORTH AMERICA

THE POCKET GUIDE TO
TREES
OF
NORTH AMERICA

ALAN MITCHELL

Illustrated by
DAVID MORE

Edited by Pamela Forey

DRAGON'S WORLD

Dragon's World Ltd
Limpsfield
Surrey RH8 0DY
Great Britain

First published by Dragon's World 1990

Editor: Pamela Forey
Designer: David Allen
Editorial Director: Pippa Rubinstein

British Library Cataloguing in Publication Data

Mitchell, Alan 1922–
    The pocket guide to trees of North America.
    1. North America. Trees
    I. Title
    582.16097

ISBN 1 85028 110 6

Series design by David Allen
Typeset by Action Typesetting Ltd, Gloucester

Printed in Singapore

Contents

Introduction 6

Introduction

There are about 700 trees native to North America. The number is not fixed as it depends on the botanist listing them and his views on which are more properly treated as full species and which as varieties of other species. The number will always be fluid as studies progress and views change. A small book like this neither wishes nor needs to include them all. Over 100 of the species are semitropical and confined to southern Florida and the southern borders of Texas, New Mexico and Arizona. Only one or two prominent or more widely planted of these can be included. Many other species are confined in nature to one or two mountain tops and where these are not spread by planting they will be seen too rarely to justify inclusion in this book.

Many hundreds of trees from other countries are planted in North America, some very widely, in streets and squares, others mainly in the bigger gardens and parks. They have no single distinction from native trees and until the observer is skilled in identification he has no means of knowing whether the tree is native or exotic. All trees are therefore selected and treated in exactly the same way in this book, regardless of their origin.

The North American sub-continent contains a range of climates and habitats, from the arctic tundra to the tropics, and from deserts to rain forests, and no species is present in every region. This book is intended for use in all regions and the trees which have been selected are those most common in each, whether the trees are native there, native elsewhere in North America, or entirely exotic. The easiest and most rewarding places in which to see a variety of good trees are Capitol Squares, city parks, cemeteries and the open big gardens; these grow a fine range of exotic trees. In native woods there is less variety and the trees are poorer, except in parts of the Alleghenies, like the Smoky Mountains, and in the Siskiyou Mountains, and in National Parks like the Olympic Peninsular and Yosemite.

Hence, treewatching is an activity available equally to those who live in cities and those in the country. This book is intended as a first step especially useful to those who travel and who can see the trees in many regions.

Abbreviations for States of USA and Provinces of Canada

Throughout the book, the states of the USA and the provinces of Canada are abbreviated. There follows a key to the abbreviations:

States of USA			
Alabama	AL	New Mexico	NM
Alaska	AK	New York	NY
Arizona	AZ	North Carolina	NC
Arkansas	AR	North Dakota	ND
California	CA	Ohio	OH
Colorado	CO	Oklahoma	OK
Connecticut	CT	Oregon	OR
Delaware	DE	Pennsylvania	PA
District of Columbia	DC	Rhode Island	RI
Florida	FL	South Carolina	SC
Georgia	GA	South Dakota	SD
Idaho	ID	Tennessee	TN
Illinois	IL	Texas	TX
Indiana	IN	Utah	UT
Iowa	IA	Vermont	VT
Kansas	KS	Virginia	VA
Kentucky	KY	Washington	WA
Louisiana	LA	West Virginia	WV
Maine	ME	Wisconsin	WI
Maryland	MD	Wyoming	WY
Massachusetts	MA		
Michigan	MI	**Canadian Provinces**	
Minnesota	MN	Alberta	AB
Mississippi	MS	British Columbia	BC
Missouri	MO	Manitoba	MB
Montana	MT	New Brunswick	NB
Nebraska	NE	Newfoundland	NFD
Nevada	NV	Nova Scotia	NS
New Hampshire	NH	Ontario	ON
New Jersey	NJ	Quebec	PQ
		Saskatchewan	SK

BROADLEAVED TREES
AND
PALMS

Black & other Willows

The **Willows** form the largest group of woody plants native to North America, with at least 90 species and 50 hybrids. There are 300–400 species worldwide, from Alaska to Chile and across Eurasia from Spain to Japan. Willow species are virtually all dioecious, that is each tree is either male or female. The flower catkins open in most species well before the leaves unfold. The willows are in the same family as the poplars but while all poplars are wind pollinated, the willows are pollinated by insects and the flowers secrete nectar to attract them. Many are good early bee plants. The seeds bear a tuft of fluffy white hairs and are carried far in the wind.

The **Black Willow**, *Salix nigra* is generally the biggest and most frequently seen willow from NB, south of the Great Lakes to WS south to TX and northern FL. In a form sometimes distinguished as the Goodding Willow, with rather smaller, duller leaves, it extends through UT and NV to northern CA. Along the Coastal Plain from VA to AL and MS and particularly around Dismal Swamp, VA, the Black Willow is abundant in roadside swamps standing behind the fringing belt of the lower, yellow-green Coastal Plain Willow, its dark-barked stems visible through the light foliage of this smaller willow and its open crown towering above it. In such places and by riversides in TX, AK and OK it is commonly 50ft tall and more. The bark of young Black Willows has coarse, overlapping plates of pink-gray. On older trees the dark bark comes away in strips. Single stems are less common than groups of three or four sprouting from a common base. The leaves are 4–6in long and the longer ones are often curved, more green and less glaucous gray beneath than in the Peachleaf Willow.

Pacific Willow

lvs

bark

Peachleaf Willow

The **Peachleaf Willow** or Almond Willow, *Salix amygdaloides* is native from MI to AB, and from eastern OR, CO and OH with outliers along the St Lawrence River. It is common beside creeks in the Prairie states and is the biggest willow to the west of them. Its bark can be nearly as dark as that of the Black Willow, but is often gray-brown, sometimes tinged with red. The leaves, narrowing rather abruptly at the apex, are glaucous, gray-green beneath. Again single stems are unusual, and two to three often spring from the same base.

The **Pacific Willow**, *Salix lasiandra* grows from central AK to southern CA and east to SK and the Black Hills, SD and can be a tree of over 60ft or low and bushy.

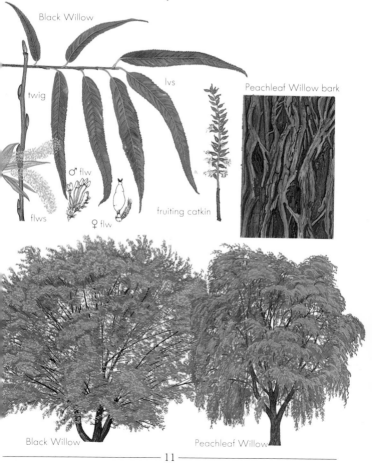

Black Willow

twig

lvs

Peachleaf Willow bark

♂ flw

♀ flw

flws

fruiting catkin

Black Willow

Peachleaf Willow

Shining & Weeping Willows

The **Shining Willow**, *Salix lucida* earns its name with its highly glossy shoots and shining leaves. It is a very hardy, tough tree growing as far north as any, from Labrador across northern ON, and MB and eastern SK to the Black Hills, SD, northern IA through OH and PA to NJ.

The **Coastal Plain Willow**, *Salix caroliniana* is a bushy plant which grows across the great expanse of the Coastal Plain from VA to TX where the roads are like low causeways, with a ditch or swamp each side. In summer it is a distinctive yellow-green with slender leaves slightly curved to nearly 4in long, somewhat blue-gray beneath. In the west this species is replaced in roadside ditches and swamps from Yukon to CA, by the **Mackenzie Willow**, *Salix mackenzieana* with shorter, broader leaves and reddish new shoots which turn shining yellow, then orange in winter and spring.

The **Weeping Willows** are a confused group with very similar trees. The true Babylon Willow is the Weeping Willow of the southern states and the others, which are hybrids with the White Willow of Europe, *S. alba*, are grown only in northern USA and southern Canada, with winters too frosty for the Babylon Willow.

The **Babylon Willow**, *Salix babylonica* is a Chinese tree. The shoots are pale yellow-green, turning olive-brown by winter and they hang in slightly longer, more slender and darker-leafed sprays than in the hardy hybrids, and the trees are usually female. This tree is grown from Philadelphia, PA and Washington, DC where it is common, along the Coastal Plain to TX and north to MO.

lvs

twig

Babylon Willow

The **Weeping Willow** of the north is *Salix* 'Chrysocoma', probably of French origin. Its shoots become bright yellow as spring approaches. It is larger and taller than the Babylon Willow, and brighter, fresher and greener in leaf. It is very common in and around towns and beside farmhouses across southern Canada and the northern USA, with big trees in OH and particularly in MI, where it may reach 80 – 90ft tall.

The **Dragon's Claw Willow**, *Salix matsudana* 'Tortuosa' is a cultivar of the Babylon Willow. It leafs out early and stays green late, often into December. It is grown in small numbers from ON to AL and IN in the east but in the west only from WA north into BC. It can grow up to 50 – 60ft tall.

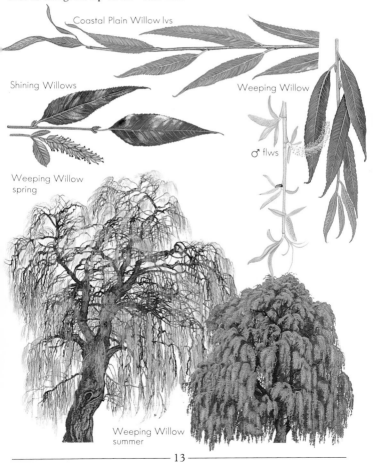

Coastal Plain Willow lvs

Shining Willows

Weeping Willow

♂ flws

Weeping Willow spring

Weeping Willow summer

Aspens & White Poplars

The poplars on this page belong to the **White Poplars**, one of the four groups into which the genus *Populus* is divided. It includes Aspens, White and Gray Poplars. These trees have a different sort of bark from that of other poplars, young shoots and branches being very smooth, gray or green, soon developing lines of small, diamond-shaped black pits. Then the bark becomes paler and at maturity it is partly or wholly white. The trees grow numerous, and often widespread suckers from their root systems. The flowers are brownish purple or gray fluffy catkins.

The **Quaking Aspen**, *Populus tremuloides* ranges across the north of the continent in a broad belt from NF to DE in the east, to the coast of AK and near the coast of BC in the west, and southwards through most of the ranges of the Rocky Mountains. Even the smallest breeze will make the leaves flutter, often audibly, caused by the slender leaf-stalks being strongly flattened. Roadside thickets are familiar features in many widely scattered areas and these stands become a spectacular brilliant gold in the fall.

The **Bigtooth Aspen**, *Populus grandidentata*, is restricted to the east, from NS to NC, west to just inside ND and southward to MO. It is more scattered in woodland than in thickets but is common beside roadsides in the middle part of its range. It has firm, substantial, bright green leaves.

The **White Poplar**, *Populus alba* is an Old World tree, introduced a long time ago. It does not grow large and it has a short life, but it suckers freely and it often forms part of shelter belts, particularly in MN, ND and the Prairie states, since it can thrive on poor sandy soils and withstand exposure. It is often mistaken for

Gray Poplar

leaf

underside

the Gray Poplar, which is more common, less bright white beneath the leaves and a much sturdier tree.

The **Gray Poplar**, *Populus canescens* is a hybrid between the White Poplar and the European Aspen and is a far bigger, more vigorous tree than either. It is used like the White Poplar but is much more common on the Coastal Plain and is the 'white poplar' seen in New Orleans and from SC to AK. It is also frequent in the west in small gardens from CO to MT.

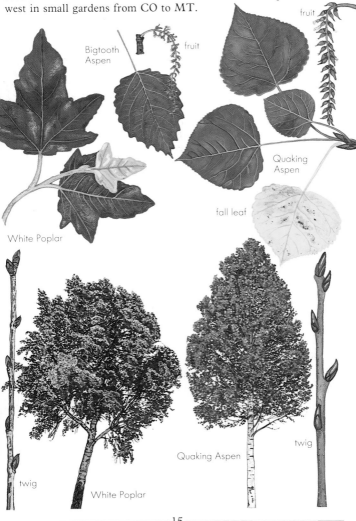

Bigtooth Aspen

fruit

fruit

Quaking Aspen

fall leaf

White Poplar

White Poplar

twig

Quaking Aspen

twig

Black Poplars & Cottonwoods

These poplars are in the **Black Poplar** group, the largest group in the genus and the one within which there is most hybridization. The chief differences between the Black Poplars and White Poplar-Aspen group are that the Black Poplars have leaves always green beneath, often paler but of similar shade to the upper side; the leaves have minutely thickened, translucent margins; the male catkins are bright or deep red and not fluffy, and the bark soon fissures into woody ridges. They also live longer and grow into trees with bigger trunks.

The **Eastern Cottonwood**, *Populus deltoides* grows across the United States east of the Rocky Mountains. Originally it grew wild the length of the Hudson Valley but was almost absent from the coast from PA to NC; it is now planted in that and many other areas in which it is not native, as far north as Winnipeg, MB. It is a fine tree with a good straight bole, often up to 100ft tall; young trees are columnar with a domed top while old ones are broad and heavily branched.

The **Plains Cottonwood**, *Populus deltoides* var. *occidentalis* can be regarded as a separate but closely allied species when it is given the name *Populus sargentii*. It is distinct in crown, bark and leaf as well as having a range to the west of the Eastern Cottonwood, but is now generally regarded as a geographical form of that tree. It occurs by riversides in dry prairie country from southern SK to NM and is often planted as a shade tree at roadside pullouts from ND to NE; it is the common poplar by creeks and roadsides in NM and through western CO into southern UT. It has been planted in

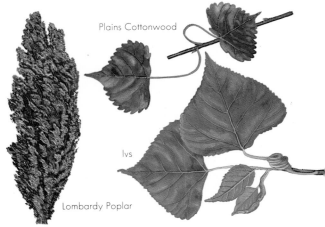

Plains Cottonwood

lvs

Lombardy Poplar

AZ around Tuba City, Flagstaff and Tucson. The tree is distinctive in its pale ridged bark, downswept outer branches bearing big brushes of upcurved shoots, and leaves with long untoothed 'drip-tips'. In October it turns bright gold.

The **Lombardy Poplar**, *Populus nigra* 'Italica', is an erect male form of the European Black Poplar which has been planted throughout the United States and all across southern Canada.

fruiting catkin

lvs

bark

twig

Eastern Cottonwood

Black, Balsam & Other Poplars

The **Fremont Cottonwood**, *Populus fremontii* is a western counterpart of the Eastern Cottonwood with the Plains Cottonwood an intermediate between them. It grows native in CO, UT, NV, NM, AZ and CA but Eastern and Fremont Cottonwoods are also planted in these areas as well. The leaves of Fremont are not as big as the larger leafed forms of Eastern Cottonwood, nor so dense. They are broader and lack the two little green glands on the stalk near the base.

Balsam Poplars are a distinct group found in N. America and eastern Asia. The buds and unfolding leaves give the group its name, for the buds are large, long-pointed and full of gummy, sweet-scented resin. The leaves open before those of other groups and they scent the air for great distances, they have stalks round in cross-section and without glands and pale, whitish undersides which often look white-painted.

The **Balsam Poplar**, *Populus balsaminifera*, formerly *P. tacamahaca*, ranges very widely from the length of the Labrador coast to northwest AK and grows along the northern tree limit all the way. In many of these northern areas it is the dominant

lvs

fruiting catkin

Fremont Cottonwood

bark

broadleaf and in the fall its clear bright yellow is the mainstay of the season's colors. It also extends southwards into the USA in many areas, especially in the mountains.

West of the Rocky Mountains is the territory of the **Black Cottonwood**, *Populus trichocarpa*, easily the biggest broadleaf in the west. Mature trees have many nearly upright, long upper branches making a narrow, ragged dome. The large, leathery, somewhat oily leaves often have crimson-stained stalks.

The fourth section into which the genus *Populus* is divided has no common name. Only one well-known member is native to N. America, the **Swamp Cottonwood**, *Populus heterophylla* from the lowlands around the Appalachian Mountains. Its large hanging leaves are all the same size, a feature of this group and in contrast to the varying leaves of Balsam Poplars. The shoots are stout and after shedding their thick hairy coating, become shiny gray or pale orange with bright red-brown, somewhat resinous buds.

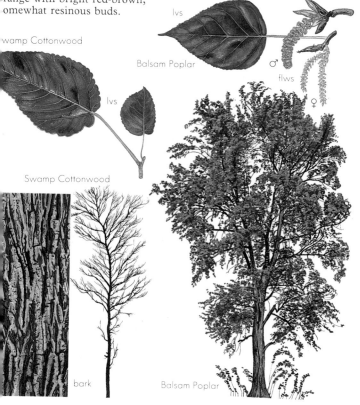

lvs

Swamp Cottonwood

Balsam Poplar

♂

flws

♀

lvs

Swamp Cottonwood

bark

Balsam Poplar

Walnuts

The **Walnuts** are a group of about 20 species found in the southwestern, central and eastern parts of the USA, Central America and the Andes, southeastern Europe and Asia. Six species occur in the USA but only two of them have extensive ranges, both in the east. They are in the same family as hickories, but whereas the walnuts and wingnuts, also in the same family, have chambered pith, the hickories do not. The stout shoots have a large core of pith, made up of hollows separated by many transverse plates. Walnut timber is fine-grained, hard and takes a high polish, which together with its fine figure and resistance to woodworm makes it valuable for furniture. In addition it is remarkably stable once seasoned and worked, and this makes it ideal for gun-stocks.

The **Black Walnut**, *Juglans nigra* is a fine tree, growing 80 – 100 ft tall. It ranges from the southern Hudson Valley and south ON to IA and eastern TX. It has been planted in southern Canada and in the west. Over much of its southeastern range it is planted with the Pecan, which it resembles. However Pecan bark grows paler and more flaky with age, while that of Black Walnut grows more ridged and darkens to black.

The **Butternut**, *Juglans cinerea* ranges from Quebec, PQ and NF to MN but is rare south of TN and MO. It is common in forests in the Alleghenies, as scattered trees which show up in fall as they lose their leaves early. It has also been planted in BC and WA. The leaves grow up to 2ft long and have dense soft hairs on the stalks and on the pale undersides.

Northern Californian Walnut

Butternut

Southern California Walnut

The **Southern Californian Walnut**, *Juglans californica* is confined as a native tree to streamsides in southern CA near the coast and on the lower San Bernardino Mountains. It forms a shrub or tree with a short trunk. The **Northern Californian Walnut**, *Juglans hindsii* is local in central CA near the coast from the lower Sacramento to the Napa Valley.

The **English Walnut**, *Juglans regia* is the only walnut with entire leaf-margins. It is native from the Black Sea to China and is found in the east from MA to OH and in the west from southern BC to NM; it is locally common in orchards in the Okanagan and in the Central Valley, CA.

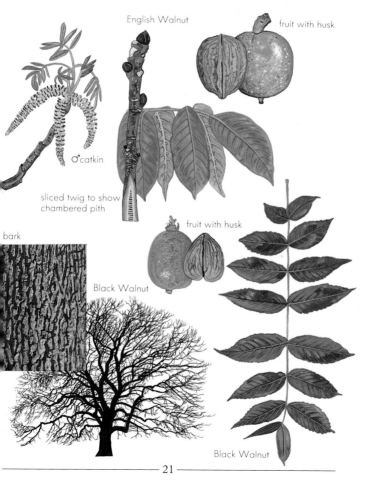

English Walnut

fruit with husk

♂catkin

sliced twig to show
chambered pith

bark

fruit with husk

Black Walnut

Black Walnut

Pecan & Hickories

The **Hickories** are a small group with 11 species in the eastern USA, another in Mexico and one or two in China. They are in the Walnut family but differ from walnuts and wingnuts in having shoots with solid pith, male catkins branched into three parts and the fruit in four segments. Their timber is very tough, elastic and shock-resistant and is used in the best axe handles and baseball bats.

The **Pecan**, *Carya illinoensis* is the finest of all the hickories as well as having the most splendid bright pink nuts. Big trees grow over 100ft tall. It is native to the Mississippi Valley, from IN and IL to TX, MS and LA but has also been planted widely across the eastern USA. It is found north to Washington, DC and all down the Coastal Plain, where in the south there are many orchards, to Pensacola, FL.

The **Bitternut Hickory**, *Carya cordiformis* is distinguished by its slender, scaly, bright golden buds, gray to brown bark finely networked in ridges and its terminal leaflet tapering to the almost stalkless base. It is native and usually common in woods almost everywhere east of the line from mid-MN to east TX, as far north as MA and the St Lawrence Valley to beyond Montreal, PQ. It is not seen much on the Coastal Plain nor is it planted noticeably anywhere beyond its range.

The **Shagbark Hickory**, *Carya ovata* has almost the same range as the Bitternut except that it does not grow on the Coastal Plain. It has shaggy bark and stout shoots, green at first then deep purple-

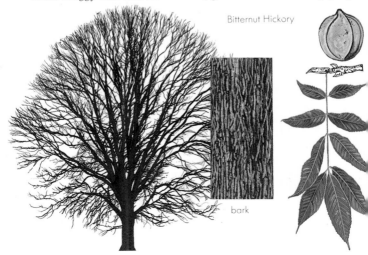

Bitternut Hickory

bark

brown. The terminal leaflet on each 5 – parted leaf is much the biggest, up to 8in long; the whole leaf is over 2ft long and has a stout 1 – 2in stalk.

The **Mockernut Hickory**, *Carya tomentosa* has smooth gray bark when young and it is still rather smoothly ridged when old. The shoots and leaf stalks are covered in hard, dense short hairs and the terminal leaflet of each leaf has a slender 1½in stalk. It has much the same range as the Bitternut but is also common on Long Island, where the twisted hanging shoots and heavy hanging leaves are noticeable.

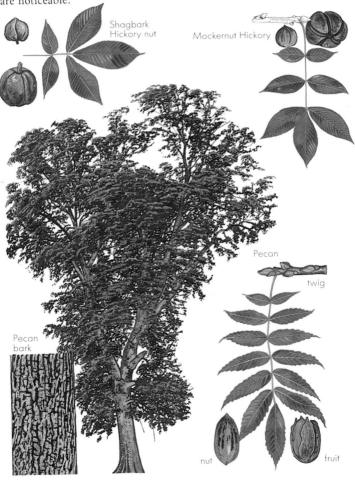

Shagbark Hickory nut

Mockernut Hickory

Pecan

twig

Pecan bark

nut

fruit

Paper, Silver & other Birches

The **Birches** are a group of about 50 species which grow round the northern circumpolar plains and to the south from FL and Spain to China. Many are only shrubs and seven are native North American trees. They are all rather similar and hybrids are frequent. The bark of most species rolls or peels off and it contains a white pigment, betulin. Birches grow rapidly when young and they are short-lived; they may die back and decay rapidly when 60 – 100 years old. They are pioneer trees, seeding on to open ground and unable to establish in shade.

The **Paper Birch**, *Betula papyrifera* extends in one form or another from Labrador and VA in the east to Yukon, western AK, WA and MT in the west, south to NE and OH. It is also called the Canoe Birch. In New England, NY, ON, into OH and PN most trees are damaged by the Bronze Birch Borer and have lost the main stem above 6 – 8ft; they grow big, upturned lower branches. The tree does not grow above 60ft tall.

The **Gray Birch**, *Betula populifolia* has very white bark with black 'Chinaman moustaches' where branches have arisen, distinctively long-tailed leaves and warty yellow shoots, turning red-brown. It grows from NS and NB through New England and NY, where it is a very common roadside and garden tree, to OH and PA where it is a local mountain tree.

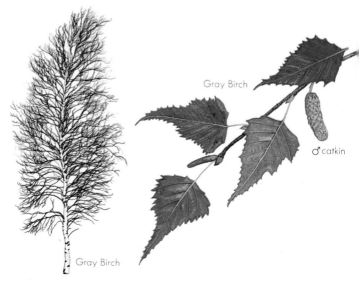

Gray Birch

♂ catkin

Gray Birch

The **European White Birch**, *Betula pendula* has long been planted in towns and gardens, across N. America, from south PQ to southern CA, but not south of PA, IN and MO in the east, except in MD and DE. It is a warty shooted birch, distinguished by its white bark with black diamond-shaped patches and by its outer crown with fine shoots hanging in tails from rising branches. The **Cutleaf** or **Swedish Birch** has whiter, less marked bark than the Silver Birch, deeply cut leaves and a narrow, long-pendulous crown. It is common on the Prairies, often grown in main streets from MB south to CO. It is also planted in southern BC and in WA.

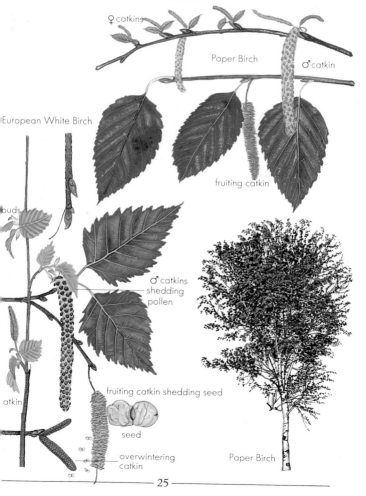

♀ catkins

Paper Birch

♂ catkin

European White Birch

fruiting catkin

buds

♂ catkins shedding pollen

fruiting catkin shedding seed

seed

atkin

overwintering catkin

Paper Birch

Yellow & Other Birches

The **River Birch** or Black Birch, *Betula nigra* has a broadly U-shaped natural distribution with the eastern arm ending in a patch in MA and CT, and the western arm threading itself up the upper reaches of the Mississippi into WI and MN. The main body of the U sweeps from MO to TX and round the Alleghenies up to NY and in the middle is a large patch in KY, TN and WV. The tree is not often planted outside its range. The River Birch lives up to its name, particularly in TX, AR, OK and in the Coastal Plain, where it is most often seen along creek-sides. This is the only birch with lobed leaves and silvered undersides to the leaves, but both features vary in intensity. Young trees have pinkish or pale coffee-brown bark with orange-brown to dark brown rough scales. Old trees can have dark purple-gray bark with orange fissures or the bark may be blackish red with small scales.

The **Yellow Birch**, *Betula alleghaniensis* shares several distinctive features with the Sweet Birch. They both have quite large, flat, many-veined leaves; hemispheric crowns of rather even-sized radiating branches; abundant fruit standing erect; and they both give off a strong scent of oil of wintergreen if their shoots are skinned and warmed. They differ in their bark and in minor details of their leaves. Yellow Birch bark is pale gray-brown with a yellow-brown tinge, flaking and peeling horizontally with tight and loose rolls. Yellow Birch occurs from NF, NB and ND through WI and MI to PA and along the mountains just into GA. Very big trees may reach 70ft tall.

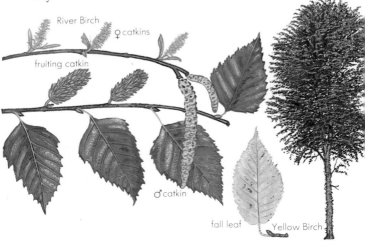

River Birch

♀ catkins

fruiting catkin

♂ catkin

fall leaf

Yellow Birch

The **Sweet Birch** or Cherry Birch, *Betula lenta* has smoky gray-black to dark red bark with purplish flakes. Its crown is less open than that of the Yellow Birch. Both trees turn brilliant gold briefly in the fall. Sweet Birch has a more southerly and easterly range than Yellow Birch, from ME to AL, south of Lakes Erie and Ontario and not west of mid-OH. Fairly big trees are common in parks and gardens, 70 ft tall and over, but it is not planted outside its range.

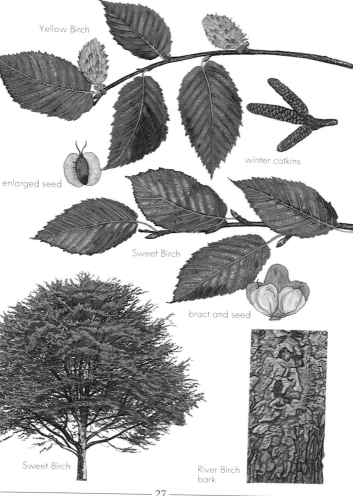

Yellow Birch

winter catkins

enlarged seed

Sweet Birch

bract and seed

Sweet Birch

River Birch bark

Alders

The **Alders** are a group of about 30 trees and shrubs of northern
temperate regions, with one species extending down the Andes to
Peru. Ten are native to N. America, of which five or so are trees
rather than shrubs. Alders are rarely more than 70 – 80ft tall
anywhere. They are members of the Birch family and they have
two highly unusual features. Firstly, their fruits not only resemble
small cones, but they ripen into hard woody structures even more
like cones, which may remain on the tree long after the seeds have
been shed. Secondly, their roots have nodules on them that house
nitrifying bacteria which take nitrogen from the air. This enables
these trees to grow on bare or made-up soils that are often short of
nitrates. European, Gray and Red Alders are planted on quarry
spoils, the banks of newly cut roads and similar places for this
purpose, however most alders grow for preference on the banks of
streams or lakes.

The **Speckled Alder**, *Alnus rugosa* has been regarded as the
extension of the European Gray Alder into N. America, but unlike
that fine tree, the Speckled Alder is little more than a shrub. It
ranges from NF to AK and south to BC, ND and NJ.

The **White Alder**, *Alnus rhombifolia* may grow up to 100ft tall,
with long slender branches drooping at the tips. It grows by
running water in the Rocky Mountains in the USA only, from ID
and MT to southern CA. The bark of young trees is pale and dark
gray and smooth, aging to dark brown, scaly plates.

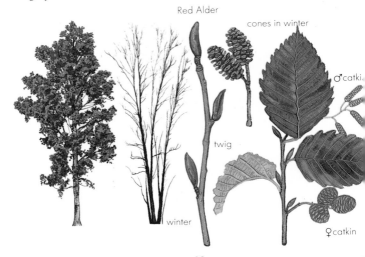

Red Alder

cones in winter

♂ catki...

twig

♀ catkin

winter

The **Red Alder** or Oregon Alder, *Alnus rubra* is the most prominent broadleaf tree in many parts of its long narrow range, close to the coast from AK to southern CA. It grows in tight groups by the roadsides in the Coast Mountain and Cascade valleys and has bark almost as white and shining as Quaking Aspen. Its large leaves, 6 x 4in, have their margins sharply turned down and the fruits are over 1in long, the largest of all the alder fruits.

The **European Alder**, *Alnus glutinosa* is naturalized from NF and PQ to PA and IL, having escaped from plantings.

European Alder

♀ flws

♂ catkins

immature cone in summer

cones in winter

Speckled Alder in winter

European Alder

Speckled Alder

Hornbeams & Hophornbeams

The **Hornbeams** and **Hophornbeams** are small to moderately large trees related to alders and birches, and now given their own family, the Carpinaceae. The hophornbeams, like the alders and birches, have their male catkins exposed and partly extended during the winter, but the hornbeams have theirs in small ovoid buds which open in mid-spring. There are 42 members of this family, 8 of them hophornbeams in which the nuts are enclosed in bladders and 34 hornbeams with the nuts in pairs on leafy bracts. Both groups range from eastern Asia across Europe and have a few species in North America. The hornbeams, with just one North American species, have leaves with numerous, prominent, straight veins, parallel from the midrib to the marginal teeth.

The **American Hornbeam**, *Carpinus caroliniana* is also called the Blue Beech and Water Beech as well as Ironwood. It has an odd distribution. From ME and PQ to MN south to TX and east to the coast all the way to northern FL is normal enough, but it is common again across the big gap to southern Mexico, Guatemala and Honduras. It is not much planted, and European Hornbeam is more common in parks. However the American species has more elegant foliage and is far superior in its orange, crimson and purple fall colors. There are hedges of it in Pittsburgh. Trees have smooth, silvery gray bark on stems fluted into rounded ridges .

The **European Hornbeam**, *Carpinus betulus* has been planted in parks and gardens from southern ON to MI and PA, especially in the pyramidal form 'Fastigiata' with a neat ovoid crown. The type is a larger tree than the American species with larger, shinier

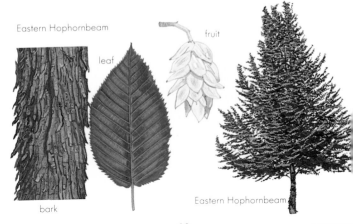

Eastern Hophornbeam

fruit

leaf

bark

Eastern Hophornbeam

but duller, coarser foliage and its new leaves are green, not orange-red. In the fall it turns yellow and dull orange.

The **Eastern Hophornbeam**, *Ostrya virginiana* has almost exactly the same range as the American Hornbeam. It has distinctive leaves, in that the teeth at the ends of the 12 pairs of veins project beyond those between them, with short whisker tips. The fall colors are pale orange and purple. The bark, cream-gray in young trees, striped buff, becomes dark brown and purple with age, shredding finely.

European Hornbeam

flws

leaf

♂ flw

♀ flw

twig

American Hornbeam

fruit cluster

leaf

American Hornbeam

European Hornbeam 'Fastigiata' in fall

Beeches

Beeches are a group of about 10 species, one in N. America, two in Europe and the rest in eastern Asia. They are mostly big or medium sized trees, often important for timber, and are in the same family as oaks and chestnuts. The male flowers are not on long catkins but in clusters on slender stalks, and the females one or two on short, stout stalks. The bark is usually smooth, pale gray, often silvery, and their buds are slender and pointed. The fruit is a woody, four-lobed involucre with hard, blunt spines, enclosing three angular nuts.

The **American Beech**, *Fagus grandifolia* is a much more elegant and attractive tree than the European Beech which is planted in parks in many places. Its bark is many shades paler gray and more silvery, and its leaves are shining rich green, 3–6in long, slender-tipped ellipses, with well-marked and regular veins in 13–16 pairs. The species has a wide range, from NS to north of Lake Huron and the south of Lake Superior, sweeping round east of IL to eastern MO, AR and TX but it scarcely enters FL. It is common in woodlands throughout and is also found in many parks, often as remnant forest but also planted. Big trees grow over 100ft tall.

The European Beech, *Fagus sylvatica* was probably one of the first trees brought to N. America, more for the quality of its timber or as a reminder of home, than for its decorative qualities. It is a coarse, dark tree, with dark gray bark on the trunk and upper branches, not so silvery as the American Beech bark. Its leaves reach 4 x 3in, have 6–7 pairs of veins and have wavy margins; they are a beautifully fresh green at first but soon darken. This beech

Copper Beech leaf

European Beech leaf

Copper Beech

an be found in Newport RI, in parts of NH, MA and OH, but grows best in the Hudson Valley. In the west it is common in and round Vancouver and Victoria. It can grow over 90ft tall.

The **Copper Beech** or Purple Beech, 'Purpurea' has brownish, black purple foliage. Large trees are frequent from ME to WI to MD and MO, notably large ones occur in the Hudson Valley, NY and in PA. It is also common in Vancouver and Victoria in the west and south into WA.

new lvs of American Beech

American Beech lvs

♀ flw

♂ flw

♂ flw detail

seed

fruit

twig

American Beech

Chestnuts & Chinkapins

The **American Chestnut**, *Castanea dentata* has fallen on hard times. Until about 1930 it was the one American species of the four natives to grow into a shapely and big tree, to 100ft tall. Since then however, it has been devastated by attacks of Chestnut Blight, *Endothia parasitica* and has joined the other three as no more than a shrub. Throughout most of its range, from ME, southern ON and eastern IN to northern GA, it is seen as sprouts from old stumps and although these grow to about 40ft, they then succumb before bearing seed. Trees planted in the western states may well escape the disease. The trees have smooth, dark gray bark until it becomes fissured into long, flat, dark gray-brown ridges flaking at the edges. The shoots are slender, shining pale yellow-green ripening to olive-brown then red-brown, finely hairy. The leaves are 6–7in long.

The true chinkapins differ from the chestnut in having woolly shoots and leaves, and only a single nut in each spiny case. The **Allegheny Chinkapin**, *Castanea pumila* grows from NJ to FL, west to eastern TX, OK and KY. The leaves are 3–5in long, unfold red with thick white hairs beneath and turn yellow in fall.

The **Golden Chinkapin**, *Castanopsis chrysophylla* grows by the coast in one locality in southern WA and from mid-OR to mid-CA in the Cascades and by the coast, with small patches in the Sierra Nevada. In OR it is a bush of the understorey and it is small in Pygmy Forest, Mendocina, CA but between these places it is a shapely, tall tree. Its pale gray bark has a few dark, sharp-edged vertical fissures. The evergreen leaves are 3 x 1in and thick and

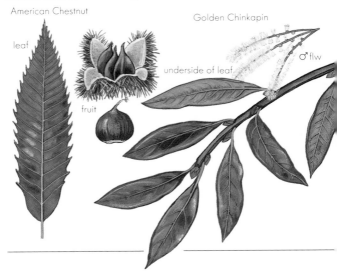

American Chestnut

leaf

Golden Chinkapin

underside of leaf

♂ flw

fruit

leathery. The flowers open at midsummer when pale yellow-green male catkins, 1–3in long, grow in big terminal bunches. Some of them bear a few female flowers near the base but mostly the females, with red-purple stigmas, grow on short catkins behind. The bright green, spiny fruits grow in tight bunches of about 10.

The **Tanoak**, *Lithocarpus densiflorus* is also a far western tree, and the only member of its genus in N. America. It grows in the Coast Range from south OR to southern CA and locally in the Sierra Nevada. It forms a bush in some places, a tall tree in others. It has large, 1in long-ovoid, pale orange to dark brown acorns in shallow, spiny cups. Young trees have whitish-gray bark but by the time they are 50ft tall the bark becomes dark brown and fissured.

Golden Chinkapin

seed

fruit

Tanoak

♂ flw

acorn

Golden Chinkapin

Tanoak

White Oaks

The **Oaks** *(Quercus)* are a huge assemblage of 450 – 500 species of the northern hemisphere, with 58 in N. America. Many are evergreen. All oaks have acorns for fruit, but their leaves vary enormously from small, thin, unlobed and untoothed to big, deeply lobed leaves with big teeth. They can be separated into five groups: White, Chestnut, Red, Willow and Live Oaks.

The **White Oak**, *Quercus alba* is typical of the group which it heads, in having rough, scaly or shaggy bark and in growing further north than all but one other oak, from PQ and ME to MN and from east TX to the Atlantic coast. It is common almost everywhere in its range. The leaves emerge stained crimson then turn cream before becoming bright green above, whitish beneath. Before falling they turn bright orange-red, crimson and red-purple. The tree may grow to 100ft or more in height.

The **Bur Oak**, *Quercus macrocarpa* is another White Oak, and it extends further north and west than any other eastern oak. It is common in woods around Winnipeg and along creeks in SD and just reaches SK and MT. It ranges to the coast in TX but is almost absent from the southeast from MS to north VA. It is the dominant oak west of Madison WI where it stands out with its dark crown, almost black branches and dark gray bole with bark deeply ridged and sometimes shaggy. It can grow over 100ft tall. Emerging foliage is a distinctive yellow. The acorns are the biggest in American oaks, exceptionally to 2 × 1½in. The leaves can be 12 × 6in and vary in depth of lobing.

The **Valley Oak** or Californian White Oak, *Quercus lobata* is confined to that state, from Trinity River to near Los Angeles. It has a short stout trunk with dark gray bark cracked into smooth, square plates, and big, curving branches, upper ones twisting to an often mis-shapen top and lower ones arching down, both with rather pendulous outer shoots.

Post Oak

leaf

bark

acorn

Valley Oak

leaf

acorn

The **Oregon White Oak**, *Quercus garryana* is the only native oak in BC and WA and extends on the Coast Range to CA. It has dark bark, blackish leaves and is often hung with mistletoe.

The **Post Oak**, *Quercus stellata* stands out wherever it is seen by the way it hangs its 4 – 8in long, seemingly cross-shaped leaves. The bark is gray-brown, finely fissured into vertical plates, flaking and stripping and sometimes shaggy. The stem is usually straight with a few, usually twisted lower branches. It is found from the coast of MA and Long Island to MO and mid-TX east to the Atlantic coast, in woods and parks.

leaf

White Oak

acorn

Bur Oak

acorn

leaf

White Oak

Bur Oak

Emory & Chestnut Oaks

The **Emory Oak**, *Quercus emoryi* is the common hillside and canyon oak across southern AZ and NM into western TX. Although it is a White Oak, it is evergreen, shrubby and not often over 30ft tall. The bark is black with gray scaly ridges, the shoots are stout, pink-brown and densely hairy, fading from the red in which they emerge. The leaves are stiff and hard, gray-green beneath, 2 x 1in. The paired acorns are nearly 1in long, smooth, bright green, ripening to rich purple-brown.

The **Chestnut Oaks** are a small group found only in eastern North America. They are characterized by large, long leaves with many shallow, usually rounded lobes or teeth.

The **Chestnut Oak**, *Quercus prinus* occurs from southeast ME and the Hudson Valley just into ON to MI and, via eastern OH and southern IL to mid-AL. On the eastern side it does what so many other trees do: it occurs along the coast through Long Island and DE and then, from around Chesapeake Bay it takes to the hills and continues to GA and AL. It has been planted on the Coastal Plain. It is a big tree, reaching 80 – 100ft tall with large chestnut-like leaves, gray-white beneath and up to 9in long. The acorns are shining rich red-brown.

The **Swamp Chestnut Oak**, *Quercus michauxii* very nearly takes over where the Chestnut Oak leaves off, to the south. They overlap in NJ and DE and then where the Chestnut Oak keeps to the hills, the Swamp Chestnut ranges through the Coastal Plain, through north FL and the Delta, LA into east TX and up the Mississippi Valley to south IN and IL, overlapping again only in the hills of GA and AL. It differs from the Chestnut Oak in having very pale, silvery or creamy gray bark fissured into small strips and flakes, and

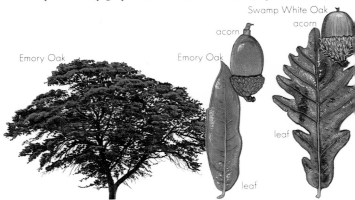

Swamp White Oak

acorn

acorn

Emory Oak

Emory Oak

leaf

leaf

leaf

leaves, darker above and more silvery beneath with more marked lobes and two more pairs of veins, to 16 on large leaves.

The **Swamp White Oak**, *Quercus bicolor* is, despite its name, a chestnut oak, not a white oak, but its leaves are much more like those of white oaks than of most chestnut oaks; usually they are 6 x 3in but they may be 10 x 6in. The bark is pale gray with a coarse network of thick blackish-gray ridges. This tree has a fragmented range from the junction of PQ and ON, the coast of ME and the Hudson Valley, east to OH and then to WI and north MO and round to OH, MD, Long Island and MA.

Chestnut Oak

leaf

acorn

Swamp Chestnut Oak

lvs

acorn

Swamp Chestnut Oak
winter

Chestnut Oak

Red Oaks

The **Red** or **Black Oaks** are another group found only in N. America, but they occur both in the east and west. They are more distinct than the other groups, with a few large teeth on the leaves which are all drawn out at the tips to whiskers, and their small acorns take two years to ripen. Their closest relatives are the willow oaks; the two groups have features in common and may hybridize.

The **Northern Red Oak**, *Quercus rubra* grows further north in the extreme east than any other oak, in NS and PQ but not as far north in the central states as the Bur Oak. It extends south to OK and AL and to the east coast from NC northwards but not on the plains of GA and SC. It is very common through the Allegheny Mountains, in OH and New England but shows up less in the south where there are so many other oaks. It is widely planted in the west, in BC, WA and OR. Many young trees have bright silvery gray, smooth bark. The bark of very wide, flat ridges and wide fissures, is typical of old trees.

The **Southern Red Oak**, *Quercus falcata* is very distinct, often a tall elegant tree, 100ft tall, with dark leaves cut into long, slender curved lobes. It is common over much of its range from NJ to north FL, west to TX and MO.

The **Black Oak**, *Quercus velutina* has a velvet-like covering of very fine hairs on the shoots, the undersides of the leaves and leafstalks. The leaves are hard and tough like parchment and the midrib tends to fork and give each leaf two outer ends. The species ranges from ME to GA in the east and from TX to WI in the west. It grows large, 70 – 100ft tall.

The **Scarlet Oak**, *Quercus coccinea* ranges from ME to AL and MO away from the coast south of VA, to over 5000ft in the Great Smoky Mountains.

leaf

Black Oak

leaf

bark

Northern Red Oak

acorn 2nd year

acorn 1st year

acorn

The **Pin Oak**, *Quercus palustris* is wild from RI and VT to KS, OK and TN but is grown widely as a city street tree far beyond its range as well as in it. It is much the commonest tree in many city parks like Central Park, New York, and in streets in both east and west. The habit of the young trees suits them to city planting, with their straight clean stem and high skirt of fine shoots below a slender spire.

The **Northern Pin Oak**, *Quercus ellipsoidalis* occurs from northern IN to mid-MN and replaces the Bur Oak as the dominant tree in parts of south MN and into WI. The leaves unfold pale crimson and turn whitish green, then shiny dark green.

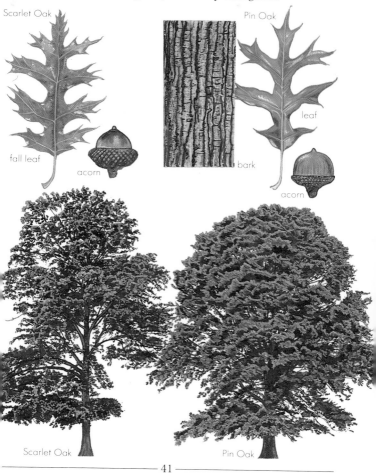

Scarlet Oak

Pin Oak

fall leaf

acorn

leaf

bark

acorn

Scarlet Oak

Pin Oak

Blackjack & Willow Oaks

The **California Black Oak**, *Quercus kelloggii* is the sole representative of red oaks in the west. It is common in most of the foothills and valleys in the mountains from southern OR to the Mexican border. In parts of OR it is a tall tree, but in parts of CA it is bushy, twisted and spreading. The bark is dull gray broken by dark narrow fissures into pale gray ridges. The leaves can be 9 x 6in and the pale green, usually hairy undersides have white midribs.

The **Blackjack Oak**, *Quercus marilandica* is an eccentric among red oaks where deeply cut, rather thin leaves are usual, since it has the broadest, most shallowly cut leaves of any oak, and they are thick and hard. They are 6 x 6in and often curl to show the underside which is pale orange with dense hairs through most of the range. The tree is rugged and broad with level branching, but a spreading tall shrub in the dry hills in TX and AR. It ranges from mid-TX to south IA and east to Long Island, NY skirting south OH and WV.

The **Water Oak**, *Quercus nigra* is a red oak with a great tendency to hybridize not only with others in the group but with willow oaks as well. It has leaves of variable shape on the same tree, from round-edged spoons to some like small Blackjack Oak leaves and others more deeply lobed. The bark is finely fissured vertically, pale or dark gray in broad, roughened plates. It is native from DE to mid-FL and TX, north to AR, TN and the plains of NC. It is common round Dismal Swamp, VA and all along the Coastal Plain and up the Mississippi Valley to TN. It can reach 80 – 100ft tall.

The **Willow Oak**, *Quercus phellos* also ranges from DE to eastern

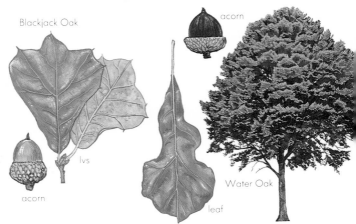

Blackjack Oak

acorn

lvs

acorn

Water Oak

leaf

TX but misses almost all GA and the mountains of NC. It is planted in the streets of New York and other cities, and generally in OH. Young trees have very smooth, gray bark. New leaves unfold late, yellow with red-tinted centers.

The **Shingle Oak**, *Quercus imbricaria* is like the Willow Oak but with leaves half as long again and on stalks three times as long. It is found almost exactly northwards from where the Willow Oaks and Laurel Oaks (*Q. laurifolia*) fade out, from AR to NJ as far as south IA, MI and the whole of PA.

Shingle Oak
acorn
lvs
leaf
Willow Oak
acorn
lvs
California
Black Oak
Willow Oak

Live Oaks

The **Live Oaks** are a small group of evergreen oaks confined to N. America, with many species in the southwest and two in the southeast. Live Oaks are in general long-lived, slow-growing trees with small, thick and hard leaves, entire or spine-toothed and rarely with noticeable lobing. The western species grow on hot sandy hillsides and in dry rocky canyons, while the two eastern species grow on the Coastal Plain on sandy, quickly draining soils, in areas with high summer rainfall.

The **Live Oak**, *Quercus virginiana* has a natural range in a belt close to the coast from VA to south TX, spreading farther inland only across peninsular FL and in central TX. In some places it is a tall tree but in other places it is shrubby. This is the tree that gives much of the character to the Plantation mansions and gardens in SC where the approach is usually by a long avenue of Live Oaks. Planting has extended the range of the species to Little Rock, AR and to the border of OK. In the east it has been planted inland in AL and in NC. The leaf shape of Live Oak is very variable in the presence of lobes and teeth, and it also varies in size from 2 to 5in long. The shoots are covered in dense gray wool.

The **Canyon Live Oak**, *Quercus chrysolepis* grows from the Siskiyou Mountains, OR southward along the Coast Range and Sierra Nevada on the mountains to the Mexican border and east in

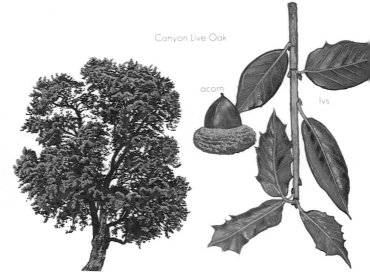

Canyon Live Oak

acorn

lvs

AZ. It is a spreading tree or shrub with both entire and spiny toothed leaves. The chestnut-brown acorns grow up to 2in long, in flat 2in cups.

The **Arizona White Oak**, *Quercus arizonica* is a Live Oak of the mountains from the western end of TX through southern NM and AZ. It is a small tree with large, twisted branches and its leaves last only one full year. They are densely hairy beneath. The bark is pale gray with scaly ridges.

The **California Live Oak**, *Quercus agrifolia* seems to have been the victim of an error in its botanical name. 'Agrifolia' means 'field-leafed' where 'aquifolia', holly-leafed must have been intended. It grows as a native tree near the coast in Mendocino County, CA, south to the border and is also frequent from the Bay area south. The bark of young trees is very smooth and black. The undersides of the leaves have tufts of hairs in the vein angles.

California Live Oak

lvs

acorn

Live Oak

acorns

leaf

Live Oak

Elms

The **Elms** are a group of about 45 species found across northern and central Eurasia and in eastern N. America. Elm flowers grow in bunches or on long slender stalks. They are all dark red, and in all but three species, two American and one Chinese (grown in America), they open well before the leaves in spring. The other three open theirs in fall.

The **American Elm**, *Ulmus americana* ranges from NS and south PQ to SK and the edges of MT and WY to central TX and FL. Although a woodland tree, this elm is most often seen in small and medium sized towns in eastern USA, in streets, squares and parks. It is also common in shelter belts. In northern woods the tree grows a sinuous short trunk bearing many sprouts and two or three spreading branches. The leaves grow up to 6in long, especially on the sprouts.

The **Slippery Elm**, *Ulmus rubra* is very widespread in the east in woods and towns, and is native from PQ to south MN, mid-MN, mid-NE and KS to east TX via north LA to the coast in SC. The bark is brown and sooty gray in coarse ridges and the rounded crown, upright in young trees, is densely hung with big leaves, up to 8in long, and looking very dark from a distance. The flowers are crowded in short-stemmed bunches, and the fruits are smooth and big, nearly 1in.

The **Rock Elm**, *Ulmus thomasii* differs from the Slippery Elm in having its few flowers in loose, open 1–2in long flowerheads and also in that the thicker shoots and small branches grow warts, then ridges and finally corky wings. The leaves are smaller, to 5in; they are bright pale green above and hairy only on the veins beneath. It is a less wide ranging tree than the Slippery Elm, although it

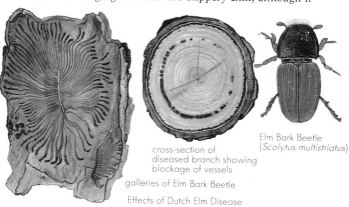

cross-section of
diseased branch showing
blockage of vessels

Elm Bark Beetle
(*Scolytus multistriatus*)

galleries of Elm Bark Beetle

Effects of Dutch Elm Disease

reaches Montreal, round the south of Lake Huron into south MN and MO and to the northern parts only of IL, IN and OH with big outliers in TN.

Dutch Elm Disease has killed many Elm trees. It is caused by a fungus which is carried by Bark Beetles. These beetles remained in the timber of Rock Elms used for the construction of small ships, in both N. America and Europe, in the 1970s, and the disease spread rapidly on both continents. Control is difficult; felling of all trees showing signs of disease is a drastic remedy but has been successful when done early.

Slippery Elm — leaf — twig — fruit — bark — Slippery Elm

American Elm — leaf — fruit — flws — American Elm

Elms

The **English Elm**, *Ulmus procera* is seen infrequently in streets
and parks in many eastern cities. English Elms are particularly
susceptible to Dutch Elm Disease since they do not set viable seed
and spread only by root-suckers. The disease can quickly run
through a population of trees which have spread by suckers.

The **Cedar Elm**, *Ulmus crassifolia* is a strange tree; its leaves are
so hard and rigidly stalked that in a wind they remain quite
unflexed and the hard, whip-like shoots bend with the leaves as one
piece. The bark is dull pink-gray becoming deeply fissured and
dark gray as the tree gets older. The tree is a small one with a short
bole, a dome of arching branches and rather pendulous outer
shoots. It is very common in TX and AR, into OK and less
common to MS and LA. The flowers appear in the fall, beginning
in August, on slender hairy stalks in heads of 3 – 5 and by October
the oblong-elliptic, deeply notched fruits, barely ½in long, hang in
masses; they are covered in soft white hairs.

The **Winged Elm** or Wahoo, *Ulmus alata* grows from TX to
central FL and south VA. It extends in bottomlands to Kansas City
then south around the Coastal Plain. It also grows in the
Mississippi bottomlands. The Winged Elm is like the Cedar Elm,
but has larger softer leaves, turning yellow earlier in the fall. The
pale gray-brown bark is prominent and less ridged.

The **Siberian Elm**, *Ulmus pumila* has long been one of the most
widely planted and useful trees in N. America. It is often, in the
semi-deserts of AZ and NM the only tree seen for scores of miles,
planted for shade at every rest-station. It is similarly planted
throughout the Prairie states to SK and as a common shelterbelt,

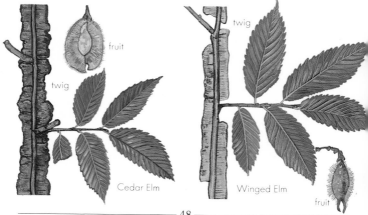

fruit

twig

Cedar Elm

twig

Winged Elm

fruit

farm and roadside tree. It is a common street tree as far north as Winnipeg, MB, and is also seen in streets in the east and west although scarce south of Washington, DC and west of the Rocky Mountains. In many places it is cut annually and grows long arching shoots sparsely set with small leaves. In others it may reach 70 – 80ft tall.

The **Chinese Elm**, *Ulmus parvifolia* is much planted in streets and precincts in south CA. It is also seen here and there in towns in the east, from New Orleans, LA to Montreal, PQ. It has a domed crown of stiffly hanging shoots. It is most like the Siberian Elm, but it flowers in the fall, has smaller, darker leaves and the bark is not ridged.

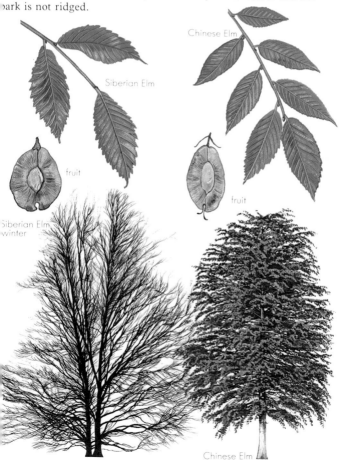

Chinese Elm

Siberian Elm

fruit

fruit

Siberian Elm winter

Chinese Elm

Hackberries & Keaki

The **Hackberries** or Nettle-trees are placed in the Elm Family but differ from the true elms in having male and female flowers on separate flowerheads on the same tree; in the fruit being a berry-like drupe, and in the bark being generally smooth although in some species it is much knobbed and flanged. There are over 50 species spread across Eurasia and North America, only seven in North America.

The **Hackberry**, *Celtis occidentalis* is the common *Celtis* species of the northeast. The main range is from RI and the Hudson Valley, NY to VA and west, avoiding most of PA and WV to MN and OK. It is a common street and park tree in many of the eastern cities. In some areas, around Indianapolis, IN and in Central Park, NY, for example, many trees are bedecked with 'witches' brooms', clusters of slender shoots which abort at the tips. The trees in Central Park have smooth, gray bark but elsewhere the bark is normally covered in dark, abrupt, broken ridges. It grows up to 70ft tall.

The **Sugarberry**, *Celtis laevigata* replaces the Hackberry from south MD and VA, around the Coastal Plain and up the Mississippi Valley to central IL and southern IN; thus the two overlap widely over northern AR and much of MO, KY, IL and IN. Sugarberry has pale ashen or pink-gray bark with short abrupt ridges, and small entire leaves, often only 2in long. It can be distinguished from Hackberry by the color of its ripe fruit, orange-red in Sugarberry and dark purple in Hackberry. Sugarberry is a common hedge tree in many areas; it can grow up to 80ft tall but in the south in small yards in cities it is often cut back and grows annual wands.

Keaki

lvs

The **Netleaf Hackberry**, *Celtis reticulata* is more or less the western hackberry, growing from ID, WA and OR to KS, CO and TX to CA, on dry hill and canyon sides. It is named from the conspicuous network of veins on the undersides of the leaves, and is usually shrubby, rarely even 30ft high.

The **Keaki**, *Zelkova serrata*, an elm relative from Japan, was sent to America in 1860 and has been much planted in parking lots and precincts from ME to DC. It is an exceptionally attractive shade tree, up to 80ft tall, and the elegant leaves turn yellow, orange and bronzy red in the fall.

twig

flws

Hackberry

fruit

new lvs of Hackberry

bark

fruit

Sugarberry

Hackberry

Mulberries & Osage Orange

The **Mulberries** are a group of about 10 species from Mongolia, China and Japan, with two in North America. The White and Black Mulberries have been cultivated for so long, for silkworm raising and fruit, that their natural ranges cannot now be defined and the Black may originally have extended into Asia Minor or even into Europe. Mulberries are deciduous trees of moderate or small size. Flowers of one sex only grow on each flower spike but both kinds of spike grow on the same tree, even if tending to be on separate branches. The fruits are peculiar in that each apparent fruit is a cluster of fruits, and the fleshy part is the swollen calyx.

The **Red Mulberry**, *Morus rubra* is found in MA and the Hudson Valley, NY and then almost everywhere south of PA and WI to mid-TX and is quite common in gardens and woods over most of this region, including the valleys in the Allegheny Mountains. It is most noticeable in the south in AL and around New Orleans, LA and in the north around Indianapolis, IN, while in MN, IA and east NE it is frequent as a roadside hedge. It can grow up to 50ft tall; trees cut back throw out shoots up to 4ft long. The leaves are late unfolding and in MN are still not expanded by mid-May. They can be 10 x 10in. The biggest leaves tend to be those cut into deep lobes.

The **White Mulberry**, *Morus alba* is a Chinese tree which has been widely planted from north NY, but not in New England, to NC and across to TX, CO and UT, NM and AZ to CA. It is less seen in OR and WA but more common in southern BC. It is common in roadside gardens in OH and PA, where it may grow

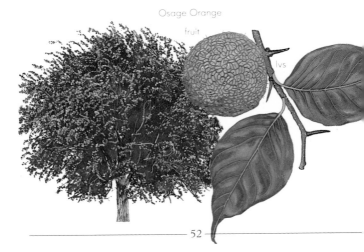

Osage Orange

fruit

lvs

into big trees 60 – 70ft tall. The smooth glossy upper side of the leaves distinguishes this from other mulberries.

The **Osage Orange**, *Maclura pomifera* is native to TX and adjacent parts of AR and OK, and it is a frequent park, garden and square tree from Toronto and Niagara Falls, ON locally to VA and DE. The bark is orange-brown with interwoven ridges which in old trees are pink-gray and stringy. The leaves vary in size greatly on the same shoot. The timber was used by Indians for bows and was superior even to European Yew.

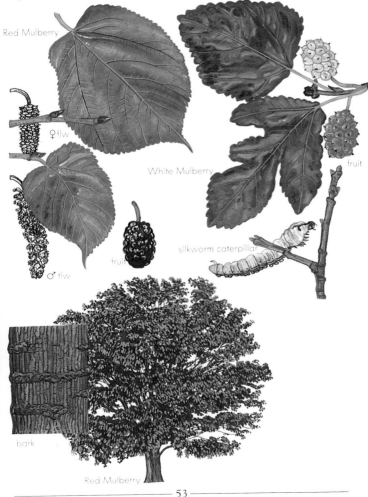

Red Mulberry

♀ flw

♂ flw

fruit

White Mulberry

fruit

silkworm caterpillar

bark

Red Mulberry

Yellow-poplar

The **Yellow-poplar**, *Liriodendron tulipifera* was thought to be the only one of its kind in the world until 1875 when the very similar Chinese species was discovered. Yellow-poplars or tulip-trees are plainly, from the curious structure of the flowers, a sort of magnolia but they differ sufficiently in their buds, shape of leaf and in their fruit to be placed in a genus of their own. The Yellow-poplar is native to nearly everywhere from MA to IN and close to the river down the Mississippi Valley to just short of the Delta and to central FL. It is common throughout the whole of this region and is usually the tallest tree in the locality, as it is in the whole region. Many trees grow over 100ft tall and the tallest reach 150−180ft high. It has been planted a little in eastern TX but widely and more commonly in AR, OK and even more in southern BC, in WA and southern CA, particularly in the streets of some parts of Los Angeles.

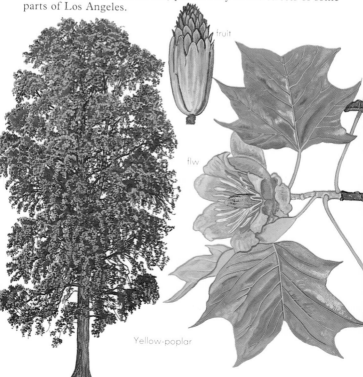

fruit

flw

Yellow-poplar

Sweetgums

The **Sweetgum**, *Liquidambar styraciflua* is only one of three members of its genus, one growing in North America and the others in Asia Minor, China and Taiwan. Its flower spikes have flowers of only one sex, the males in 3in terminal spikes, and the females in solitary globular clusters on 2in stalks in the leaf axils. The flowers of both sexes grow on the same tree, although some trees have only a few females while others are crowded with them. The fruits are hard and woody and hang dark brown on the trees through the winter. A leaf crushed or torn emits a strong sweet, aromatic scent.

The tree ranges from Long Island, NY to east TX and mid-FL and is common almost throughout, but it is dominant in east TX and AR. It is planted in MA and ME, around Victoria and Vancouver BC, around Seattle and coastal WA and in Los Angeles, CA. The color display in fall is prolonged. In TX and AR, this tree provides the mainstay of the fall colors, and before turning scarlet and deep red, many trees are mottled orange and scarlet.

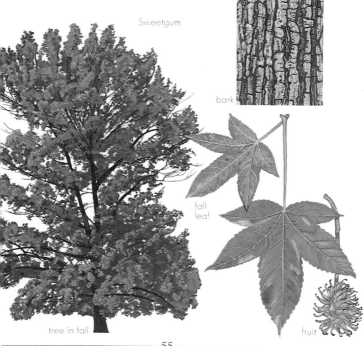

Sweetgum

bark

fall leaf

tree in fall

fruit

Sassafras

The **Sassafras**, *Sassafras albidum* is a tree in the Laurel family, a group specializing in aromatic foliage, and is only one of three species of Sassafras in the world, the other two being in China and Taiwan. It ranges from mid-ME to mid-MI, south IL and MO to east TX and central FL. It often spreads by suckers from the roots and runs along the edges of roads and fields, making long hedges with trees at varying distances holding up umbrella crowns on twisting branches. This is most often seen in parts of PA and in AR. There are almost none planted in the west. Hedgerow sprouts have predominantly pale orange bark, while the bark of older trees has pale orange or red-brown ridges broken into big blocks by ashen-gray fissures. In SC and GA, Sassafras forms an undergrowth in the woods and is a good tree only in towns and gardens. The fall colors are spectacular, as the leaves turn through yellow and orange to scarlet and crimson. Male and female flowers are usually on different trees and the fruits grow in threes or fours on erect, red stalks ripening into clear red berries. The leaves vary in shape from unlobed leaves to asymmetrically two-lobed leaves, like mittens, and to quite deeply three-lobed leaves; the variation may occur on the same tree, but older and less vigorous trees and shoots bear unlobed leaves. This is not a tall tree and heights of 80 – 85ft are unusual.

Sassafras

fruit

bark

winter tree

California Laurel

The **California Laurel**, *Umbellularia californica*, also belongs to the Laurel family. It has highly aromatic foliage; the aroma from crushed leaves is spicy and pleasant but over indulgence is paid for by a sharp headache. Nonetheless the leaves can be used to flavor stews. The California Laurel is native to the Coast Ranges from OR all through CA and on the western flanks of the Sierra Nevada, and in the southern cross-ranges. It tends to be small with many stems growing from near the base, at least in woods which have been cut over, but is known to reach 150ft tall when by itself.

California Laurel

bark

fruit

Magnolias

The **Magnolia** family is divided strictly between the Americas and eastern Asia, with 10 of its species in the Americas. One grows in northern South America, one in Mexico and eight in the USA, one extending just into Canada. In the flowers of Magnolias, there is no true distinction between sepals and petals. All American magnolias flower when in full leaf, while most from China open theirs well before the leaves unfold, and they are pink and white flowers so it is these trees which are planted for early spring color.

The **Cucumbertree**, *Magnolia acuminata* ranges into Canada, just into ON and keeps largely to the hills from there to GA and in MO and AR. Its leaves are sometimes 1ft long and silvered beneath. The scarlet seeds, typical of magnolias, protrude on white stalks from the bright pink-purple fruits. The variety, *cordata*, the Yellow Cucumbertree, is wild only in GA but has been planted in gardens north to MA.

The **Sweetbay**, *Magnolia virginiana* is deciduous in the north of its range, in MA, on Long Island, NY and along the Coastal Plain, and evergreen in the south, by the Gulf Coast to south FL and east TX. It is highly attractive in fall where miles of the slender shrubby trees line the roadsides, as around Dismal Swamp, VA, with shiny green and bright blue-white foliage surrounding the 2in scarlet fruit. It is much planted in OH and MI. Although usually 30ft or less, it can reach 60ft in height.

The **Southern Magnolia**, *Magnolia grandiflora* has the biggest flowers of any native tree, up to 10in across, and with a strong

Southern Magnolia

flw

fruity fragrance. Although native only to the southern states from NC to TX, on the plains, it is planted northwards to DE and PA, OH and IL, also in southern CA.

The **Umbrella Magnolia**, *Magnolia tripetala* has big leaves, up to 20in long, tapering to the stalk and prominently veined. The flowers are white and 6in long. Native to the mountain valleys from PA and OH to GA and to the coast in VA and NC and the hills of AR and OK, it is also planted in gardens in ON.

The **Saucer Magnolia**, *Magnolia* x *soulangiana* is a hybrid between two Chinese species. It is the common garden magnolia, flowering early and freely even when young. 'Lennei' is a form with larger, darker leaves and superior flowers.

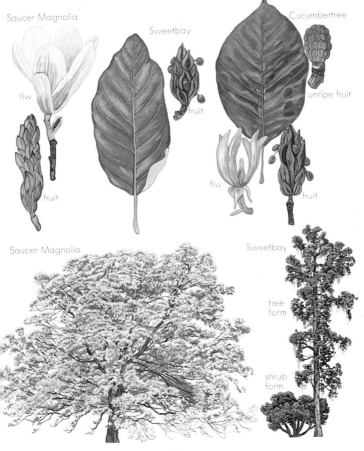

Saucer Magnolia

Sweetbay

Cucumbertree

flw

fruit

fruit

unripe fruit

flw

fruit

Saucer Magnolia

Sweetbay

tree form

shrub form

Sycamores

The **Sycamores**, the sole members of the family Platanaceae, are also called Planetrees and Buttonwoods. The Sycamores are large to very large trees and long-lived, with male and female flowers in separate heads on the same branches. The timber is hard and dense, with a beautiful figure of dark freckles in a cream to pink background. There are three species in North America, one in Europe and Asia Minor, and about four in Mexico and Central America, but the hybrid London Plane is the most widely planted.

The **Sycamore**, *Platanus occidentalis* grows wild by streams and in damp soils on the plains and in the mountains from ME through southern ON, MI and WI to IA and eastern TX. It is planted in city streets in all parts of this range and a little beyond in the west. This large tree grows up to 150ft tall and has a very open crown, blue-white bark on the branches and scaly orange-brown bark on the bole. In summer the clusters of new leaves emerge white among the dark green foliage. Fully open leaves measure 10 x 12in. In the fall the leaves turn from bright orange to orange-brown.

The **California Sycamore**, *Platanus racemosa* grows from the Upper Sacramento River along the lower Sierra Nevada and in the Coast Range from Monterey to Mexico. It differs from the Sycamore in having about five small fruits strung down the stalk and leaves with three deeply cut main lobes, either entire at the margin or with small, peg-like teeth.

The **London Plane**, *Platanus x acerifolia* is a hybrid between the Sycamore and the Oriental Plane, *Platanus orientalis*. It is long-lived and has a remarkable tolerance to polluted air and bad rooting conditions. It is common in cities in the northern USA, in New

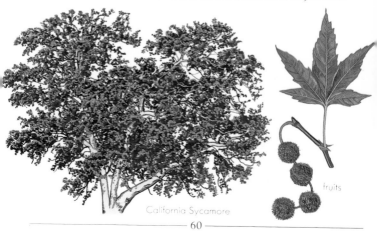

California Sycamore

fruits

England, NY, OH, PA and MI, and in southern BC. It often becomes too big for its position and its roots lift many sidewalks. It differs from the Sycamore in the variably deeply 5 – lobed leaves, brown and yellow bark and having 4 – 6 fruits on a stalk.

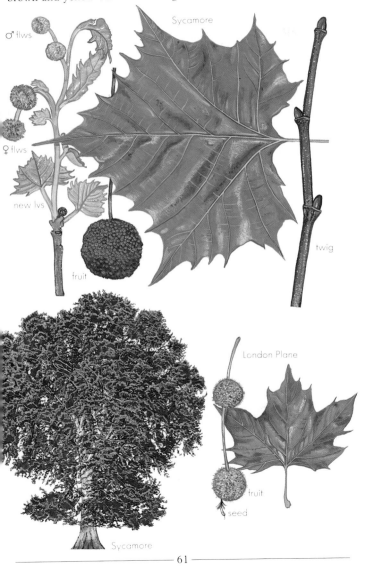

Hawthorns

The **Thorns, Hawthorns**, or Crataegus species, are in the great Rose family; 35 species are recognized with 46 hybrids. They are long-lived and decorative in flower and fruit, making good park and garden trees, as well as stockproof hedges.

The **Downy Hawthorn**, *Crataegus mollis* has downy undersides to the leaves, as well as downy shoots and fruits. In one form, the Arnold Hawthorn from MA and CT, the spines are 3in long and the shoots become bright orange-brown; this form is often planted. The Downy Hawthorn grows wild from NS and PQ to AL and TX west to ND. It is common in city parks in eastern cities. It is a small tree, growing to 30ft tall.

The **Cockspur Hawthorn**, *Crataegus crus-galli* is among the most spectacularly thorned species, with close rows of curved, 2–5in, pale brown spines. It occurs at wood-edges or in open, low woods from southern PQ, ON and WI to MA, northern FL and GA to TX. It is also planted occasionally in towns and gardens. The bark is brown or pale gray in thin plates, crumbling to orange. The flowers and fruit-heads are without hairs, unlike those of its hybrids like the Plumleaf Thorn.

The **Black Hawthorn**, *Crataegus douglasii* is a largely western species with a curious range from AK to north CA, a broad arm across to WI and MI and another in the interior Rockies to NM. Spines are often absent and when present are only 1in long. The fruits are ⅔in long and black.

The **Washington Hawthorn**, *Crataegus phaenopyrum* is an attractive little tree, unusual in the wild from VA to FL and AR to IL, but it has escaped from cultivation from OH to MA and is planted frequently in cities in the east.

The **One-seed Hawthorn**, *Crataegus monogyna* has long been introduced and is so easily raised, useful as a stockproof hedge and

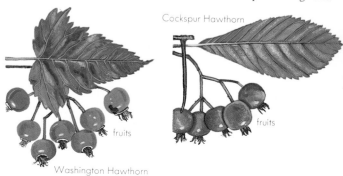

Cockspur Hawthorn

fruits

fruits

Washington Hawthorn

hardy, that it has been spread and then seeded itself across wide areas from PQ to NC, OK and NE and in OR and BC. It is planted in many city parks.

Paul's Scarlet Thorn, *Crataegus oxyacantha* 'Paul's Scarlet' is widely planted in ON and New England and particularly in the west, in MT, ID, WA and BC.

Downy Hawthorn

thorn

fruits

flws

Black Hawthorn

fruits

twig

thorn

Black Hawthorn

summer

Paul's Scarlet Thorn

Mountain-ash

The genus *Sorbus* is divided into two remarkably differently foliaged groups, and one of hybrids between them, variously intermediate. The **Mountain-ash** group has large compound leaves with a dozen or more leaflets; the Whitebeam group has simple rather rounded leaves, as do the hybrid Service Trees. Although so diverse in foliage, *Sorbus* is maintained as a genus because of similarity in the flowers and fruit. The genus is in the Rose family and has the usual 5–parted calyx and five petals. The flowers are usually white and they are fragrant, pleasant to most people but sometimes bordering on the offensive. The majority of the 100 plus species are Mountain-ashes from eastern Asia. There are seven native to North America, four of them shrubby. The Whitebeams are confined to the Old World, and therefore so are the hybrids.

The **American Mountain-ash**, *Sorbus americana* is scarcely more than a shrub and the European species is preferred for planting in parks and gardens. The American one is also known as Roundwood and grows into a round-topped, spreading low tree seldom 30ft tall, with pale gray, scaly bark. It has resinous winter buds, dark red above and greenish beneath, glossy with a few long, silky gray hairs, on stout, red-brown hairy shoots. The leaves are up to 8in long, usually with 13–15 leaflets but sometimes only with 7. In the fall the leaflets turn orange and the stalks bright red. It is found from NF to Chesapeake along the coast, along the Allegheny Mountains just into GA, through MI and WI to southeastern MB.

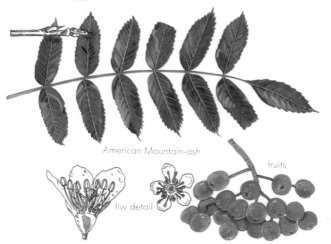

American Mountain-ash

flw detail

fruits

The **European Mountain-ash**, *Sorbus aucuparia* is wide ranging over the cooler parts of Europe and Asia. It grows rapidly into an upright tree, sometimes over 60ft tall, but is not long-lived. The bark can be silver-gray but in the north it is often coppery-brown; it is smooth until net-worked by a pattern of shallow, scaly ridges. The leaves usually have 15 leaflets. This tree is common in parks and gardens from Montreal, PQ to BC and south roughly to OR, CO, OH and PA.

The **Showy Mountain-ash**, *Sorbus decora* is so named because of its splendid heads, 6in across of large, ½in berries. It is, in effect, a northern and high-altitude form of the American Mountain-ash, occurring over much the same range but not extending south beyond MA, NY and northeast IA and occurring further north in NF, PQ, ON and Labrador.

European Mountain-ash

flws

fruits

'Fructo-lutea'

twig

European Mountain-ash

bark

Crab-apples

The **Apples** are medium-small trees of the cooler parts of the northern hemisphere. They are typical tree-members of the Rose family in having numerous intergrading variants and hybrids. But unlike most of the others, the genus *Malus* has not been found to cross with any other genus, nor will it graft readily onto any of them. Many wild species bear occasional thorns. The trees are mostly very hardy, tough and able to grow in difficult soils, and of great value in city street planting.

The **Sweet Crab-apple**, *Malus coronaria* grows wild from NY and IL to AR and GA along streams and woodland edges. It has red-brown bark, shallowly fissured into broad, scaly ridges. The flowers are scented more strongly in the double-flowered form 'Charlottae', which is planted in parks and gardens.

The **Prairie Crab-apple**, *Malus ioensis* is the mid-western Sweet Crab from IN and WI to OK and AR. It is a low bushy tree with level branches which have leaden gray bark, while that on the trunk is in narrow, brown strips. The shoots are dark red with a gray bloom. This tree is planted in gardens in WI, MN, south to CO. A far better garden tree is the form, Bechtel's Crab, 'Plena' which bears abundant double pink flowers; in full bloom it looks more like a Japanese Cherry than an apple.

The **Japanese Crab-apple**, *Malus floribunda* was brought from Japan in 1862 and is a common tree in town gardens from ON to DE in the east and in CA. It comes into full leaf very early, but in May the pink and white flowers smother the crown, followed in some years by tiny yellow fruits.

Bechtel's Crab

Bechtel's Crab

The **Purple Crab**, *Malus* x *purpurea* is a hybrid raised in France. It has dark red pigment in all its parts, is very hardy, and is valued for its amenity value in cold northern areas and also as a pollinator in orchards. It has been selected and crossed with other species so that a great array of red to purple-leaved hybrids is now widely planted.

The fastigiate **Pillar Apple**, *Malus tschonoskii* is particularly useful for planting in streets and narrow plazas because it is neat, with brilliant fall colors, exceedingly resistant to poor soils; and it bears few and small fruits, a useful point in streets.

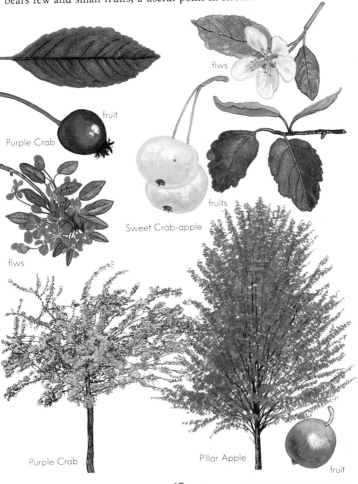

flws

Purple Crab

fruit

flws

Sweet Crab-apple

fruits

Purple Crab

Pillar Apple

fruit

Serviceberries & Loquat

The **Serviceberries** are small trees and shrubs in the Rose family, closely related to Hawthorns and the Mountain-ashes. Although only a small group, with between 2 and 16 species in Eurasia and North America, they show many variations and hybrids in the wild and in cultivation.

The **Downy Serviceberry**, *Amelanchier arborea* is usually a shrub with light brown or gray-brown, very smooth bark and slender, sharp buds. The flowers are profuse unless the plant is shaded, and all open within a few days. The bloomed, dark purple-red berries are soon eaten by birds. It grows from southern SF to MN south to LA and FL. The **Western Serviceberry,** *Amelanchier alnifolia* forms shrubby thickets from AK and Mackenzie to north CA with a band across NE and MN to ON and PQ. It differs in its much more coarsely toothed and round-tipped leaves and ovoid buds.

The **Loquat**, *Eriobotrya japonica* from China and Japan is also in the Rose family, an evergreen too tender to be grown outside the warmest, most frost-free regions. It makes a broad-topped tree to 30ft tall. It has few, stout shoots with big dark, crinkled but shiny leaves, up to 1ft long. The flowerheads are 6 x 8in covered in dense brown hairs and the edible fruits ripen in spring, after the late summer flowering. The tree is frequent in small gardens, courtyards and on walls from Charleston, SC to LA and TX, and less frequently to AR. In the west it is found in CA.

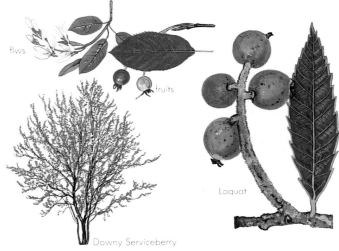

flws

fruits

Loquat

Downy Serviceberry

Pears

The **Pears**, *Pyrus* are an Old World group, widely grown for their large fruit with a peculiar texture deriving from grit-cells. The **Common Pear, Pyrus communis** is an upright tree with a long straight trunk and dark brown bark broken into small squares. It can be over 60ft tall and is long-lived, with very strong, durable and finely grained timber which turns well and makes excellent fuel. Like all pears, its flowers open as the leaves are only beginning to unfold. In this one the leaves are then pale yellowish brown, partly hidden by the large flowerheads which open fairly early in spring.

The **Bradford Pear** is a selected form of the Callery Pear, *Pyrus calleryana* from China. This has become one of the most useful trees in city plantings, in precincts and streets from ON to GA. The neat, dense, upright, ovoid crown is held on a trunk with pale gray smooth bark, darkening with age and becoming lightly fissured and scaled. The shoots are brown with a bluish bloom. The flowers are white, with broad rounded petals in a large head, opening among silver-haired, unfolding leaves which in the fall turn yellow, then bright orange-scarlet. The tree is prominent in many cities in the east from Toronto southwards to LA and OK.

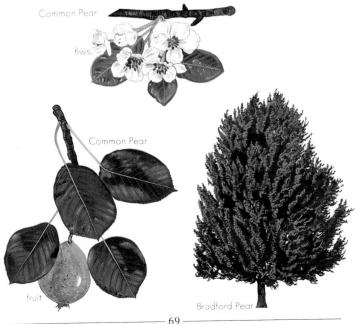

Common Pear

flws.

Common Pear

fruit

Bradford Pear

Cherries & Almond

The genus **Prunus** includes cherries, plums, almonds, apricots, peaches and cherrylaurels, as well as bullace, sloe and damson. They all have the basic Rose family flowers with five sepals and five petals, but differ from other members of the family, in having a fruit with a single seed, the hard central 'stone'. This is surrounded by thick, fleshy more or less edible tissues in all except the almonds in which it is dry and stringy. The majority of species are medium-small, mostly short-lived trees. In North America there are 18 native species, some of them shrubby and 5 more have escaped from cultivation. The cherries grown for fruit derive mainly from the Mazzard and the Sour Cherry, *Prunus cerasus* naturalized widely in Europe and western Asia but not known wild.

The **Black Cherry**, *Prunus serotina*, is in the birdcherry group with the flowers in spike-like racemes at the ends of leafy shoots. The bark of this tree is dark purplish gray, peeling in curved strips and ageing to brownish-pink, broadly fissured. The leaves are 5in long and have waved, thickened margins. In the fall most of the leaves turn clear bright yellow. This tree is native to the region south of a line from NS to MN and east around Houston TX, but scarce from SC to AL. It is common in woods and is often planted within its range.

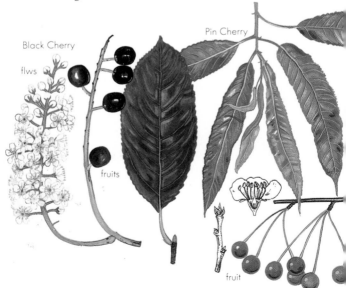

Pin Cherry

Black Cherry

flws

fruits

fruit

Chokecherry, *Prunus virginiana* is another birdcherry like the Black Cherry, and is almost a shrubby version of it. The tree has a remarkable range, all across Canada from Labrador to BC and across the USA south to Chesapeake, TN, MO and NM to CA. It is often seen on roadsides.

The **Pin Cherry**, *Prunus pensylvanica* is usually a shrubby tree with bright red shoots. It is found almost all across Canada and southwards in mountains to GA in the east and CO in the west.

The **Almond**, *Prunus dulcis* when grown in orchards for its fruit, is often a white-flowered form. For decorative planting the larger rosy-pink flowered forms are grown.

Almond

fruit

flws

Almond

flws

fruits

Chokecherry

Almond

Cherries & Plums

The **Mazzard**, *Prunus avium* is the Gean or Wild White Cherry of
Europe. It is one of several species from which eating cherries
derive, but its fruits are small and are eaten by birds before
ripening fully. It is a tree of great amenity value, for its clouds of
white flowers in late spring, and its yellow, orange and crimson
leaves in late fall. The growth pattern of the tree is highly unusual,
with the branches confined to whorls at the ends of each year's
growth, until it becomes broadly domed with age and the outer
shoots hang. This tree has escaped from cultivation and has become
naturalized in many regions; it is also planted in parks and gardens.
It is particularly common in southern BC.

The **Double-flowered Mazzard,** 'Plena' has dense rows of
flowers opening two weeks later than the single-flowered form and
lasting a week or two longer. It can be 80ft tall, unlike the slightly
more opulently flowered, similar, double white Japanese Cherries,
which flatten out at 25ft.

The **Myrobalan Plum**, *Prunus cerasifera* is the first spring-
flowering tree in bloom, starting in January or February, with its
green leaves opening at the same time. The little plums are edible.
This species is rarely planted but can form suckers where it has
been used as an understock.

A common variety of it is **Pissard's Purple Plum,** 'Pissardii',
which is found in the suburbs of cities, especially in the western
USA and BC. It has a rather shapeless crown, with brownish-red or
muddy purple leaves following the rather pretty, starry white
flowers which open from pink buds. A much improved variety,
'Nigra', has shiny, dark red leaves and pink flowers. The flowers
open a week later than those of the Purple Plum and last longer.

Weeping Higan Cherry   Pissard's Plum 'Nigra'

The **Sargent Cherry**, *Prunus sargentii* may grow up to 50ft tall and it provides a great display of massed, rather small flowers in spring and another of scarlet foliage very early in the fall. It is grown mostly in New England, from ME to DE and less frequently in parks, in Vancouver, BC and Seattle, WA.

The **Higan** or **Rosebud Cherry**, *Prunus subhirtella* is common only as the Weeping Higan Cherry, 'Pendula' sent from Japan in 1862. It is common in MA, CT, NY and PA, OH and DC and often 60ft tall, a fountain of delicate pink in March. It is grown in the large gardens and parks in BC and is frequent in WA.

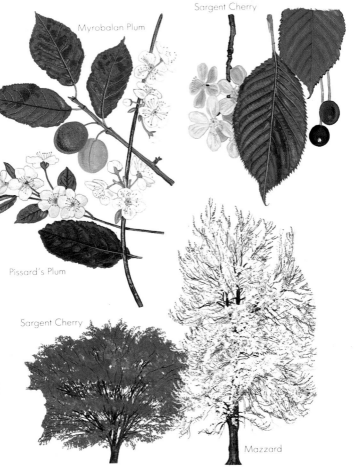

Myrobalan Plum

Sargent Cherry

Pissard's Plum

Sargent Cherry

Mazzard

Japanese 'Sato' Cherries

The **'Japanese' Cherries** were produced over a long period some 300 years ago in an old tradition of crossing and selecting among decorative plants in Japan, with some also from China. There are no records of the parentage of these trees but the bristle-tipped teeth on their leaves derive from the Oshima Cherry, *Prunus speciosa* and the copper red-brown young leaves of many of them are from the Hill Cherry, *Prunus serrulata* var. *spontanea*. All Japanese Cherries are grafts, usually low down and grow heavy spreading branches. They are relatively scarce in North America but may be found in parks and gardens from PQ to MD in the east, especially in ON and New England, OH and PA to MI and WI and in BC, WA, ID and MT in the west with a few in OR and CA.

'Kanzan' is probably the commonest cherry in N. America. The strong rising branches drooping with years of being bowed down by the weight of the superabundant flowers, and the pale, whitish green undersides of the leaves identify it in summer. Fall color is amber, pink and red.

'Taihaku' has an extraordinary history and exists by the wildest chance. Known only from a silken embroidery in Japan dating from about 1750, it was the lost 'Great White Cherry'. In 1923 a woman took the flowers from a dying tree she had bought in a job-lot from Japan in 1900, to a show where Collingwood Ingram was a judge, in Sussex, England. He took what shoots he could to make grafts and four years later was shown the embroidery in Japan, and was told the tree was lost 200 years ago. He said he had one in his garden in Kent and then sent some buds by air to be matched with the embroidery picture. Every 'Taihaku' in the world derives from that dying tree. The flowers can be 3in across and the hard, dark leaves 8in long. It is a strong-growing tree with stout branches.

The first 'Sato' to come into flower is **'Shirotae'** with its large

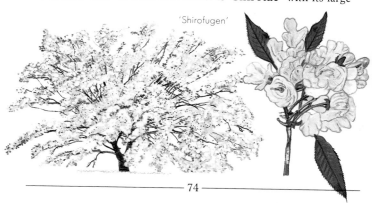

'Shirofugen'

single and semi-double flowers among bright green leaves. The leaves together with its flat crown identify the tree in summer. It is planted in Botanic gardens and parks in NY, Victoria and Seattle.

'Shirofugen' is among the last to open its flowers. The flowers open pink among dark red leaves, then turn white, striking beneath the large leaves, then as these turn green the flowers go pink again and last a long time. This tree makes very strong growth, soon level then drooping at the branch ends. It grows in Botanic gardens in WA, NY and ON.

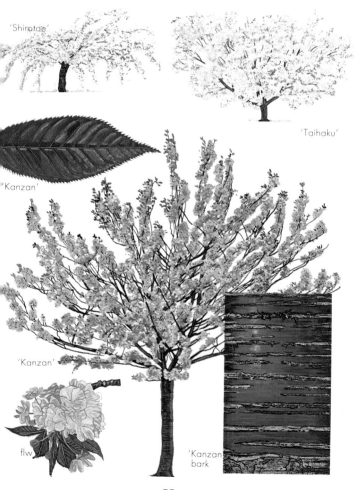

'Shirotae'

'Taihaku'

'Kanzan'

'Kanzan'

flw

'Kanzan' bark

Redbuds & others

The Pea family is a huge one, uniting all the plants in which the fruit takes the form of a legume, a pod with the seeds arising along one margin and splitting along both sides when dry. It includes all peas and beans, lupins, locusts, wistaria and redbuds, many with edible fruits and seeds and some highly poisonous. Stature varies from tiny herbs, through bushes like Gorse and Broom, to very large trees.

The **Eastern Redbud**, *Cercis canadensis* is an upright, bushy crowned, flat-topped small tree on a short, slender trunk, seldom much more than 30ft tall. The tree ranges from south NY, south MI and IA to TX and everywhere to the east except FL, and is a fairly common woodland tree over much of that area. It is also common in gardens, notably in OK, AR and along the Gulf Coast. It is planted in large gardens north of its range in ON and MA, and as a street tree in some places. From PA to NC, increasingly from north to south, it is attacked by a canker and many branches hold dead, brown leaves in summer.

The **California Redbud**, *Cercis occidentalis* is a shrub, rarely 20ft tall, with deep red-purple shoots and smaller leaves often notched at the tips. It grows from south UT and NV through CA to AZ.

Voss's Golden Chain Tree, *Laburnum x watereri* 'Vossii' is a handsome hybrid tree with long chains of yellow flowers; it is a popular garden tree, commonest in ID, WA and BC.

The **Silk Tree** or Mimosa, *Albizia julibrissin* is a southern Asiatic, low spreading tree popular in small roadside gardens where the winters are not too severe. It is grown from Long Island, NY,

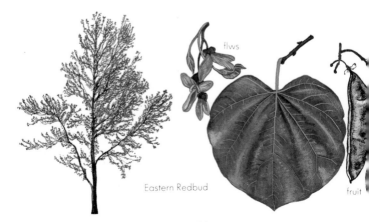

flws

Eastern Redbud

fruit

in the Coastal Plain, TX and north into MO and IL in the east, and north to Seattle in the west. These roadside garden trees are about 25ft tall, very flat-topped with big branches. They are often pruned back annually. The bark is dark, greenish-gray, striped vertically with prominent brown speckles. The leaves are 12 – 18in long and turn dark gray-green in late summer then yellow and orange. The flowers have the scent of sweet hay and open throughout the summer.

The **Chinaberry**, *Melia azedarach*, from India and China makes a low rounded crown densely set with 2ft dark leaves. It is common in small gardens from GA to TX and AR, north to TN. The bark is purple-gray with fine, pale brown fissures. The single bony seeds in the fruits have been used as beads.

Chinaberry

flws

fruit

Voss's Golden Chain Tree

fruit

flws

Silk Tree

flw

fruit

Silk Tree

Locusts & Pagoda-trees

The **Locusts**, *Robinia* are a small group of suckering trees and shrubs native only to Mexico and the USA. They have two spines at the base of each leaf, and some species have soft, clammy spines in great numbers on new shoots.

The **Black Locust**, *Robinia pseudoacacia* is the biggest species and has become by far the most widespread. The bark of young trees and of vigorous suckers is smooth, bright brown, which soon becomes fissured and matures to dark dull brown or pale gray, networked by deep broad ridges. The leaves unfold yellow and towards the end of summer are dull, gray-green, often scorched by early frosts in the north, to dark gray before being shed. The timber is extremely strong, durable in the soil and hence valued for fence posts. It was once sought after for ships' masts and a form, var. *rectissima*, Shipmast Locust cultivated for this purpose because it has a good, straight trunk, is still seen from NJ to New England. The natural range of Black Locust is now even less meaningful than that of most trees in North America, as it is far more common almost everywhere else. It was in the Appalachian Mountains from mid-PA to GA and AL and in the Ozark and Ouachita Mountains of AR into MO. Most of this area has been cut over and the trees are grown-on suckers, several from a stump, or are bushy at high altitudes. Better trees grow in parks and gardens further north, where it might reach 90ft tall. It is common from PQ everywhere to the south. In the west it is running wild in the lower Fraser Valley, BC and is abundant in the Okanagan Valley and around Victoria and Vancouver. It is also common in WA, ID and MT, UT and NV.

Pagoda Tree leaf

Pagoda Tree

Weeping Pagoda-tree

The **Pagoda Tree**, *Sophora japonica* comes from China and Korea. Somewhat like the Black Locust, the Pagoda Tree has a more open, spreading crown and less deeply ridged bark. Its blue-green shoots lack spines, the leaflets on its leaves are pointed and the big, open flowerheads stand at the shoot tips in September. The leaves emerge white. This tree is much planted in squares, parks and streets from south ON to VA and west through MI and OH to MO and in BC and WA. Big trees grow up to 90 – 100ft tall.

The **Weeping Pagoda Tree**, 'Pendula' makes a mound, sometimes 40ft tall, of contorted branches from which the outer shoots hang. It seldom flowers.

Black Locust

fruit

flws

Black Locust

Honeylocusts & others

The **Honeylocusts** are some of the few members of the huge Pea family which have ordinary shaped flowers with 3 – 5 petals, instead of the peaflower with standard, wings and keel. They are remarkable for the branched thorns growing from the trunk. Two of the world's 14 species are native to the USA.

The **Honeylocust**, *Gleditsia triacanthos* usually has bunches of ferocious thorns fairly thickly spread on its trunk, but a thornless variant, 'Inermis' also occurs in the wild. This is fortunate for the Honeylocust is invaluable in tolerating the heat, dust and drought of downtown city streets and it is planted among skyscrapers from Montreal, PQ and Toronto, ON, GA and Seattle, WA. Its native range is only from PA along the western flanks of the Alleghenies to AL and TX and north to New England.

The **Kentucky Coffee-tree**, *Gymnocladus dioicus* also has nearly regular flowers but with the sexes on separate trees. Male flowers, on 4in spikes, are white and green striped in bud, opening to 5 – petalled, starry white flowers with orange anthers. Female flowers, about 50 on bright green racemes 10 – 15in long, open greenish-white and cup-shaped in a ribbed, dark red calyces. The leaves can be 45in long and 25in across, and unfold late and pink, turning white then green, then yellow and orange before being shed, the main stalk persisting many days longer. Native from west NY and PA to TN and east OK, NE and SD it is seen more in parks and gardens beyond its natural range than in woods. Big trees reach 80 – 100ft tall.

The **Tree of Heaven**, *Ailanthus altissima* from north China, has

Kentucky Coffee-tree

Tree of Heaven

been planted in almost every city in North America from Montreal, PQ to Victoria, BC and Charleston, SC to Los Angeles, CA. Only parts of OR, north CA and south FL seem to be relatively free of it. In many cities, like Washington, DC and Memphis, TN it ramps around the inner suburbs, seeding and suckering in sidewalks, medians and yards and it runs wild in the Allegheny Mountains to 2500ft, only curbed by the frost. Male trees have large panicles of flowers, red in bud and opening after midsummer to cream, unpleasantly scented, 5 – petalled flowers. Female trees have 12 x 12in panicles of flowers, becoming big bunches of scarlet winged fruits, turning brown and hanging late, well into winter in the south.

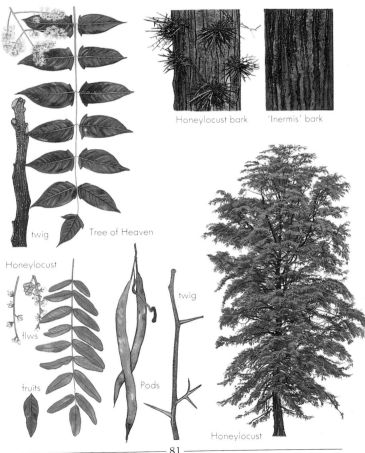

Honeylocust bark

'Inermis' bark

twig   Tree of Heaven

Honeylocust

flws

fruits

Pods

twig

Honeylocust

Hollies & Box

The **Hollies** comprise several hundreds of species from both hemispheres. There are 13 species in eastern North America, mostly very small trees. Hollies are mostly evergreen with hard, firm leaves, but a few are deciduous, two of them in North America. Unlike most plants in which annual leaf-shedding is a defense against severe winters, the deciduous hollies tend to be found in the south and the most northerly ones are evergreen. The leaves have a thick cuticle covered in wax which gives the surface a high polish in several species. Male and female flowers are usually on separate trees.

The **American Holly**, *Ilex opaca* grows wild in patches by the coast from MA to Long Island, NY and inland in southeast PA and more commonly and widely spread from NJ to mid-FL and east TX north through AR and TN to WV. It is a common roadside tree, up to 50ft tall, in western LA and through eastern TX into AR and grows in many places from VA to GA. The bark is smooth dark gray, finely striated with dark yellow-green.

Of the other American hollies, the **Yaupon**, *Ilex vomitoria* is a very small tree that ranges on the Coastal Plain from VA to TX and north into AR and OK. The leaves persist for two years on pale gray shoots arising from stout, level branches. The **Dahoon**, *Ilex cassine* spreads on the Coastal Plain from NC to LA, mostly on swampy land. It is a low shrubby tree with roughened, dark gray bark and densely silky shoots.

The **European Holly**, *Ilex aquifolium* is hardier than all but one American species and is planted each side of the US-Canadian border but cannot survive the winters of PA, DE or NJ and is common only in the west, on the coast of WA, OR and CA. Many

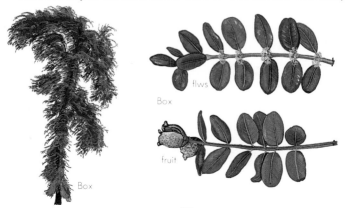

flws

Box

fruit

Box

Box

varieties are grown in parks and gardens. The 'Golden Milkmaid' is one of many similar forms with spiny, pale yellow blotched leaves. The Yellow-berried Holly has yellow berries and the Hedgehog Holly, 'Ferox' has rows of spines on the upper surface of the leaves. The Weeping Holly, 'Pendula' and Perry's Weeping Holly are both female, pendulous forms.

The **Box**, *Buxus sempervirens* from Europe, is a member of a small genus not native to N. America. Around public buildings and in parks there are bushes, often trimmed. The wood is the only temperate wood more dense than water, it is very hard and used in making precision instruments and blocks for woodcuts.

'Golden Milkmaid'

'Hedgehog Holly'

Yaupon

Dahoon

♂ flws

♀ flws

fruits

European Holly

American Holly

Sugar & allied Maples

The **Maples** are the equal of the oaks in their ubiquity in North America, their value as timber, ornament and amenity, and the diversity of their foliage and bark. They are however, fewer in number, with 13 species native to North America and about 150 worldwide. They have opposite leaves and fruit while the flowers are either in catkin-like racemes or in umbels.

The **Sugar Maple**, *Acer saccharum* has the most vibrant orange-scarlet fall colors of any maple and is very common as a woodland and town tree over its range from south PQ, NS to MN and IA south to MO and in the mountains to TN and NC where it reaches 4300ft. It may reach 140ft tall in the wild and many Main Street trees are nearly as big.

The **Black Maple**, *Acer nigrum* is very closely related to the Sugar Maple, with larger darker leaves more thinly spread over a more open crown, turning rich yellow in the fall. They can measure 6 x 9in on 6in stalks and they have soft hairs on the underside. The Black Maple has a similar range to the Sugar Maple but is less common and does not extend so far north. It is a big tree, growing up to 80ft or more in height.

The **Canyon Maple**, *Acer grandidentatum* is a smaller tree than its close relative, the Sugar Maple. It is a tree of damp canyons in the southern parts of the Rockies, from the ID/WY border south through east UT and CO to NM, AR and Mexico.

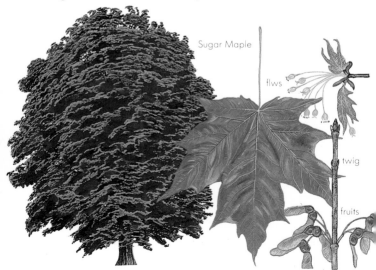

Sugar Maple

flws

twig

fruits

The **Norway Maple**, *Acer platanoides* ranges through northern and central Europe to the Caucasus. It is quite like the Sugar Maple, and is often planted with it in streets. The Norway Maple has smooth, very finely fissured bark becoming shallowly networked by ridges, where the Sugar Maple has coarsely scaling bark becoming platey and shaggy. The sap of Norway Maple is milky, not clear; the flowers have prominent yellow petals and are in umbels which come out before the leaves. Norway Maples are common street trees from PQ to WI south to MD and frequent from there to GA and AL with fewer in OK, AR and IA. In the west it is frequent in WA, ID and MT.

'Crimson King' is a variety of the Norway Maple; its leaves have a rich ruby-red color when the sun shines through them, as they have dark red undersides. The name is often mistakenly given to the duller 'Goldsworth Purple', which has bigger leaves, purple on top and dull green beneath. It is common in PA, OH, IN and IL but ranges into PQ, ON, ME south to GA and west to SD, MT and UT. It is also seen in BC and WA.

Sugar Maple

fall leaf

fruit

Norway Maple

Black Maple

'Crimson King' leaf

Planetree & other Maples

The **Planetree Maple**, *Acer pseudoplatanus* is the Sycamore of England and 'Plane' of Scotland. It is not native to either country but to continental Europe. Brought to North America long ago, it is, like some other European trees which are reputed to be common in northeastern USA, really common only in Newport and Middleton, RI. Elsewhere it is no more than locally frequent in NY, PA and DC in the east. It is difficult to understand why this coarse tree with negligible fall colors is planted when there are many superior native species. It is however, imperturbably robust in the face of smoky air, sea winds and poor soils, and grows very fast in youth. Planetree Maple timber is white, bone-hard and strong. It neither stains nor takes up the taint from food.

The **Silver Maple**, *Acer saccharinum* shows why it was given that name when a gust of wind displays the undersides of its leaves. The silver undersides remain when the leaves change color in the fall, to yellow and biscuit, with some reds. The flowers open about two months before the leaves and the fruits are shed in early summer. Planted in streets where the summers are hot, the bark is smooth and silvery gray. On old trees it is dark, flaking and shaggy and trunks bear numerous sprouts. The native range is from NB and south PQ to NY, then in the hills to MS, west to AR and ND, but it is a common street tree beyond this to east TX, CO, NM, UT, NV, ID, MT and particularly in WA and BC. The biggest trees are in parks within its natural range, where it may reach 90 – 100ft tall.

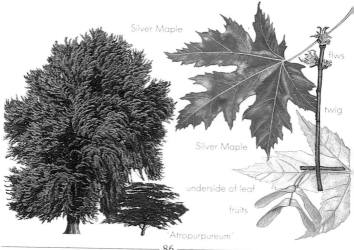

Silver Maple

flws

twig

Silver Maple

underside of leaf

fruits

'Atropurpureum'

The **Smooth Japanese Maple**, *Acer palmatum* was brought out of Japan in 1820. These slow-growing trees are popular for planting in even the smallest yards and are common from south ON and New England to OH and, less commonly south to GA and from Vancouver southwards. There are many forms of this plant. 'Atropurpureum' and similarly colored forms, with purple leaves are often grown. The best form is 'Osakazuki' with large green leaves above scarlet fruit in summer and blazing scarlet foliage in fall, even in shade.

The **Fullmoon Maple**, *Acer japonicum* grows into a bigger tree with many upright, smooth gray stems and 1in purple flowers in nodding bunches before the leaves unfold fully. Its form, 'Vitifolium' grows up to 40ft tall and has bigger leaves turning gold, scarlet, crimson and purple in the fall.

'Vitifolium'

Planetree Maple

fruits

twig

Planetree Maple

Fullmoon Maple
'Vitifolium'

Boxelder & other Maples

The maples show great diversity in their leaf-shapes. While the majority have 3 – 5 main lobes each with teeth or minor lobes, some have no lobes at all. But one species has more than three leaflets, and may have up to seven. This is the **Boxelder**, *Acer negundo*. It has an extraordinary native range, from NY south of the Great Lakes, sweeping north to central MB, SK and AB then southeast to TX with large areas in the eastern and central Rocky Mountains from MT to NM and AZ. This maple has the sexes on separate trees and the flowers open before the leaves. The male trees have 5in long, beard-like bunches of slender threads. Female trees have only 6 – 10 flowers in bunches which are also 5in long. The fruits hang brown after the leaves have fallen.

The **Rocky Mountain Maple**, *Acer glabrum* is a low bushy tree in western woods. It normally has leaves divided into 3 varying lobes but occasionally leaves have 3 leaflets. It grows from MT and SD to NM and AZ and in the Sierra Nevada, CA; another form of it grows from AK to WA, OR and MT.

The **Red Maple**, *Acer rubrum* is named for its early spring show of bright red flowers on bare shoots. The fruits which follow mature rapidly and are shed before midsummer. Fall color can vary from bright gold to purple and scarlet, but often the hillsides appear scarlet for miles. The Red Maple has a greater north-south range than any other North American tree, from the eastern end of NFD to very near the southern tip of FL. Westward it crosses south PQ and mid-ON to WI and southwards it curves to exclude

flws

fruits

Boxelder

Boxelder

MO and IL and swings back to east TX. It is most abundant in wet lowland areas. It is commonly planted in cities and towns throughout its range and to a smaller extent in the west.

The **Striped Maple**, *Acer pensylvanicum* is one of the Snakebark Maples, the only one native to North America. This small group of maples is distinguished from all the others by their red shoots which are thickly striped with white before maturing into green; by their gray bark which is patterned with chalky white stripes; and by their stalked buds and long racemes of flowers usually of one sex. The range of the Striped Maple extends from NS and PQ along the coast to VA, along the mountains to GA and west to MN, but it is rarely seen west of the Alleghenies.

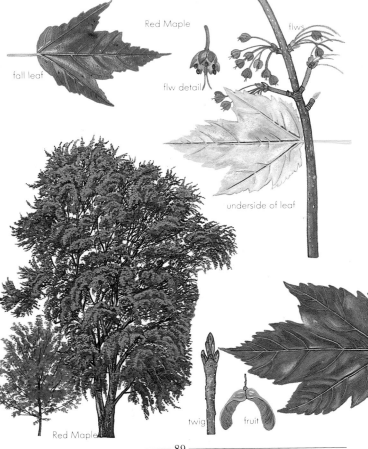

Red Maple

fall leaf

flws

flw detail

underside of leaf

twig

fruit

Red Maple

Horse Chestnuts

The **Buckeyes** are a group of about 15 species of botanically very distinct plants of the northern hemisphere, with 6 species and 11 natural hybrids in the east and one species in the west of North America. They have opposite leaves and buds; compound leaves of 5 to 7 leaflets which radiate from the tip of a stout stalk, making a palmate or digitate leaf; flowers in terminal panicles and fruit containing a single seed or two large, smooth seeds in a leatherys husk. In Europe these trees are called Horse Chestnuts, referring to the seeds as being coarse, and inedible, unlike those of true chestnuts.

The **Horse Chestnut**, *Aesculus hippocastanum* is confined as a wild tree to a few mountains between Greece and Albania and was unknown to botanists until 1596. It was rapidly planted all over Europe and was an early colonist in North America. It differs from all the American buckeyes in its shiny orange-brown, glutinous terminal buds, bigger leaves with completely stalkless leaflets, 1ft tall heads of predominantly pure white flowers and very prickly husks around the glossy, grained mahogany seeds. Each flower opens with a broad splash of yellow near the base of each petal and once the flower has been pollinated by a bee, this turns rapidly orange, then crimson. Although this is a spectacular tree in flower, it is dull in summer and unreliable in its gold or red fall colors, so it is astonishing that in a land of such superb trees as the Yellow Buckeye, its hybrids and others, the Horse Chestnut should be planted anywhere except in a few parks. But it is almost the only species planted at all in streets and in some entire regions. It is a common street tree from ON and VA to IA and WI and from MT and ID to BC, and is most common in RI and MA, also down the west coast in BC and WA.

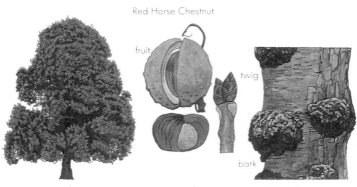

Red Horse Chestnut

fruit

twig

bark

In Europe probably, and before 1820, the Horse Chestnut crossed with the Red Buckeye to give the hybrid **Red Horse Chestnut**, *Aesculus* x *carnea*, a tree with coarse, dark foliage and dull flowers. It develops big cankers on its twisting branches and eventually falls to pieces. No organism has been found in the cankers. The tree breeds true, unlike most hybrids, because of spontaneous doubling of the chromosomes, probably in the original tree. It is common from ON and NY to MN, in southern BC and northern WA. The fruit husks are nearly smooth, and each contains dull, dark seeds, often three.

Horse Chestnut

flws

twig

fruit

Horse Chestnut

Buckeyes

The **Buckeyes** or American Horse Chestnuts consist of six species; one which keeps itself to itself in the far west and the others in the east, which can be sorted into 5 species, one variety and 10 hybrids or about a dozen species.

The western species is the **California Buckeye**, *Aesculus californica* which grows in the low, dry foothills from Shasta to the Coast Ranges, south along the western slopes of the Sierra Nevada. It is an odd little tree with low branches spreading from 1 – 3ft up the trunk, scaly, thick, pale pink-gray bark and very resinous red-brown buds. The leaves are yellowish in summer and black in fall. After the leaves have fallen, the fruits remain prominent and pink-brown for weeks.

The **Yellow Buckeye**, *Aesculus octandra* is the finest of the group. It does not quite achieve the massive stem or broad crown of the European Horse Chestnut, but it can be taller, and has elegant bright foliage and brilliant fall colors. It is remarkable that the Yellow Buckeye is so little planted in parks or streets. The shoots are shining gray-buff with a few small pale lenticels and the 4 – 8in long, finely toothed leaflets have stalks from 1 – 2in long. The species ranges from southwest PA and south IL in valleys and on hills in the Alleghenies just into GA. Big trees grow over 100ft tall.

The **Red Buckeye**, *Aesculus pavia* is only a small tree, often little more than a shrub with a slender crown of rising branches and, in the open, pendulous outer shoots, but in flower it puts the Red Horse Chestnut to shame. The slender panicles, 5 – 8in long, holds flowers which are a good bright dark red without the muddy tone of those of the ordinary Red Horse Chestnut, and the leaflets

Ohio Buckeye

fruit

winter

are shining dark green. It is native to the Coastal Plain from south NC to mid-FL and TX, inland in AL and up the Mississippi Valley to OK, MO and IL.

The **Ohio Buckeye**, *Aesculus glabra* has much the most extensive range of the buckeyes and is like the European Horse Chestnut in having leaflets with scarcely any stalk, and fruit husks with short spines. The flower panicles are 5in long and hairy, densely set with flowers in bunches of 5. Its range extends from west PA to TN in the Allegheny valley bottoms and from IL and IA to west AR and, as Texan Buckeye, var. *arguta*, through mid-TX. It is planted in city parks and squares within its range.

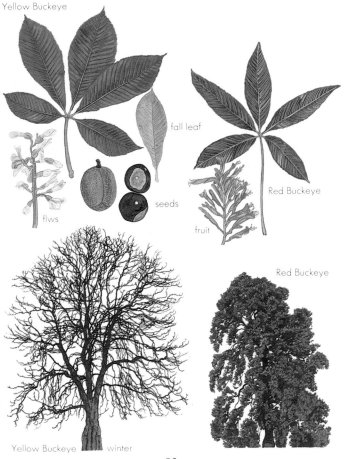

Yellow Buckeye

fall leaf

Red Buckeye

flws

seeds

fruit

Red Buckeye

Yellow Buckeye   winter

Basswoods & Lindens

The **Lindens, Basswoods** or **Limes**, are a group of some 30 species around the northern temperate region with, like the elms, the exception of western North America. There are three species native to eastern North America. They are all deciduous, alternate-leafed, medium to large trees requiring damp, quite rich soil. The flowers are perfect and in little bunches spreading from about half way along a stalk that grows half way along a leafy bract.

The **American Basswood,** *Tilia americana* is distinguished by its apple-green buds and shoots and the prominent series of parallel pale veins on each glossy leaf. The leaves are almost the same color beneath as above, normally some 8 x 7in but on sprouts and young trees they may measure 15 x 12in. The native range of this tree is extensive, from NB north of Lake Huron to southeast MB and east SD in the north and from east KS and north AR, TN and the highest ranges in NC in the south. In the east it reaches the coast from MB and NJ, then keeps to the hills to NC. Within its main range and to some extent beyond it to the west and north, it is a universal town and city tree. Big trees may reach 80 – 100ft tall.

The **White Basswood,** *Tilia heterophylla* is closely related to, and overlaps in range in parts, with the American Basswood but is, from a distance rather more like the Silver Linden because of the white undersides of its leaves. It also has many more flowers in each bunch than the American Basswood, up to 25, and lacks the gloss and rich green of the upper sides of the leaves. In the hills of WV, the silver flashes on the windblown leaves in the roadside woods. The range extends south to AL and has outliers in MO. It is also planted in cities in the range.

White Basswood

fruit

The **Silver Linden**, *Tilia tomentosa* comes from the southeastern parts of Europe, the Caucasus Mountains and Asia Minor. It is a very sturdy, fast-growing tree with a regular, hemispheric, domed crown. The shoots are covered with dense white down until the summer when it wears off. The oblique leaves measure 5 x 4in, crinkled and thick, densely covered beneath in gray-white hairs. The margin is often curled up. The flowers are late and highly fragrant. This is an infrequent tree in city parks from ON and PA to OH, with a few in NC, IA, MO and IL. In the west it is scarce from BC to CA.

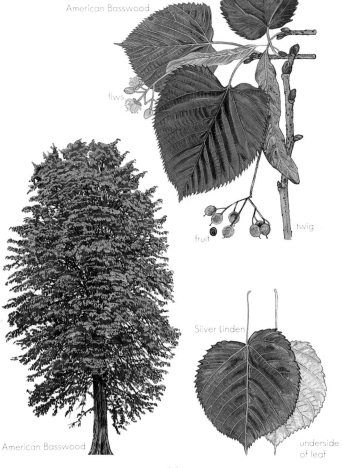

American Basswood

flws

American Basswood

fruit

twig

Silver Linden

underside of leaf

Basswoods & Lindens

The **Small-leaf Linden**, *Tilia cordata* is native to Europe and the Caucasus. It has small, nearly round leaves and abundant bright yellow starry little flowers which, instead of drooping beneath the bracts as in other common basswoods, spray out at various rising angles. It has been widely adopted as a street tree in American cities, from PQ to WI south to NE and VA. It is also frequently seen in BC and WA. A recent selection in North America is 'Greenspire' with an extra neat, conical crown and orange shoots. This is much planted now, particularly in ON, OH and IA. It is very hardy.

The **Broadleaf Linden**, *Tilia platyphyllos* from Europe and Asia Minor, has leaves no larger or broader than those of the European Linden, and in one form they are considerably smaller. The leaves are distinct, however, in being softly hairy all over, with harder, larger veins beneath, and at least until late summer, the leafstalks and shoots are variably densely hairy. This is a cleaner tree than the Small-leaf and European Lindens, and rarely has any sprouts around the base or on the trunk, making a fine domed, often hemispherical crown. It flowers before any other basswood, with large, pale flowers, three to five hanging from each prominent, large and pale bract. It is locally frequent from ON to mid-VA and OH, and uncommon west to St Louis, MO. In the west it is frequent in BC.

The **European Linden**, *Tilia* x *europaea* is a hybrid between the Broadleaf and Small-leaf Lindens and has a strong tendency to large bunches of sprouts around the base and on burls on the trunk. The untidy growth distinguishes the tree in winter from the American Basswood. It is said to be common in North America, but this must

bark   Carolina Basswood   fruit

be from a failure to separate it from the Small-leaf Linden, which is at times labelled 'European Linden'. It is in fact common, like several other European trees, only in Newport, RI.

The **Carolina Basswood**, Tilia caroliniana is a species widespread across the south, extending from the NC coast and foothills to TX, OK and AR. It has rusty brown hairs beneath the leaves.

flws

Broadleaf Linden

fruit

'Greenspire'   Small-leaf Linden

Tupelos & others

The **Tupelos** are a small group related most closely to the dogwoods. They conform to the pattern exhibited by so many genera, in which there are species native to eastern North America and Mexico and to eastern Asia but none anywhere between them. Of the 10 species, five are trees and three of these are American.

The **Black Tupelo** or Blackgum, *Nyssa sylvatica* is the only wide ranging species of the three. It is native to woods from ME and the ON shore of Lake Erie to TX and mid-FL, and common in hills over much of its range. Its fall colors begin as mottled yellow, orange and red, before becoming scarlet. Its craggy bark and elliptic leaves are like those of Sourwood which grows to a similar size in the same woods from PA southwards, but that has finely toothed leaves while those of Black Tupelo are entire, and smooth and glossy. They are 2 – 5in long generally, but some of 7in long may be found, usually on the frequent suckers. Male and female flowers are on separate heads but on the same tree. Black Tupelo is often planted in parks from NY to TN. It may grow up to 70 – 80ft tall.

The **Water Tupelo**, *Nyssa aquatica* differs from the Black in its longer leaves, more tapered at the tips and in its single female flowers. It ranges from Richmond, VA to Houston, TX and up the Mississippi to Cairo, IL.

♂ flws   ♀ flws

fruit

Tupelo

The **Golden Raintree**, *Koelreuteria paniculata* from eastern Asia has 12–16in long, widely branching panicles of flowers and bright pink or red, 2in bladder-like fruits. This tree is widely planted in parks and squares from Newport, RI and MA to SC, TN and AR, most commonly on the Coastal Plain and in OH. It is also frequent in towns on the Pacific coast. On the Gulf Coast it is largely replaced by the **Formosan Golden Raintree**, *Koelreuteria formosana*, a tree with more doubly compound leaves, 20–30in long and dull purple-red fruits.

The **Dovetree**, *Davidia involucrata* is also called the Ghost or Handkerchief Tree. It is related to ivies, dogwoods and tupelos but is now accorded a family of its own. It was discovered in 1869 in China. The most common form of this tree has shiny smooth green undersides to the leaves and purplish bark. It is this form which is seen in collections in MA, NY and PA and also in parks and gardens in BC and WA.

Golden Raintree

fruit

Dovetree

flower

bract

Golden Raintree

Dovetree

Eucalyptus Trees

The **Gumtrees** or Eucalypts are the dominant trees in Australia but are absent from New Zealand. Although confined as natives to Australasia, they are now grown in almost every warm country in the world. There are about 600 similar species. These aromatic, evergreen trees set no winter buds and grow continuously in climates with no cold period. They have juvenile foliage of broad, opposite leaves, often clasping the stems, but nearly all soon grow alternate, slender, adult leaves. The flowers are enclosed in hard capsules with lids that open to let bunches of stamens protrude.

The **Bluegum Eucalyptus**, *Eucalyptus globulus* from Tasmania was introduced into San Francisco in 1875. Flowering and seeding throughout the year, and with seedlings growing 6 – 8ft a year, this very aggressive species escaped into the hills to the south and has taken over extensive areas to 2000ft. Its northward spread has been stopped only by hard frosts; it extends some 80 miles into OR near the coast.

The **Longbeak Eucalyptus** or Red Gum, *Eucalyptus camaldulensis* is unique in its natural range, from coast to coast across northern Australia. It is less hardy than the Bluegum and likes hotter summers so it ranges less northwards in CA, only to the Bay area, but further east, into AZ where it is common in many cities. It is a tree of much less dark and heavy aspect than the Bluegum, its adult leaves being 5 – 6 x 1in, pale green with a white midrib, against 8 – 10 x 3in and dark blue-green in the Bluegum. It is not unlike a willow. The flowers grow in bunches of 5 – 6, globular in bud with stout beaks; fruits open out to brown, 5 – pointed stars. In Bluegums, the solitary flowers ripen to big, top-shaped capsules, bloomed blue-white and falling to carpet the ground beneath, providing instant recognition.

Silver Dollar Tree

The **Silver Dollar Tree**, *Eucalyptus polyanthemos,* from New South Wales and Victoria, Australia, is the only gum seen in the eastern states outside southern FL. It is uncommon from Atlanta, GA to west of New Orleans, LA and from near Yuma to CA. In inland GA and AL it is often cut to the ground by frost and re-grows as a bush, bright blue-white with round, opposite leaves. Adult foliage is similar with alternate leaves.

juvenile lvs

adult lvs

Longbeak Eucalyptus

Bluegum Eucalyptus

Silver Dollar Tree

Bluegum Eucalyptus

Dogwoods

The **Dogwoods** are a group of about 40 mostly temperate area trees ranging across North America, Europe and Asia of which 14 trees and shrubs are American.

The **Flowering Dogwood**, *Cornus florida* is by far the commonest one for its wide natural range from Portland, ME south of IL to east TX is extended by planting, including south BC and north WA. Within its range it is a common woodland tree and a very common town and garden tree. It makes a bushy, open, upswept low crown and grows slowly to no great age so it achieves no great size. The square-blocked red-brown bark is highly distinctive and a useful feature in separating this and the otherwise similar Kousa Dogwood, especially in winter. In these dogwoods the large 'flowers' consist of a central boss of minute true, four-petalled flowers, surrounded by showy 2in bracts, usually four in number. These are usually white in Flowering Dogwood, but the form *rubra* has soft pink bracts and is often favored for planting and is the commoner form in the west. The glossy bright red berries are at their best when the leaves are turning through white and pale pink to become curled and rich dark red.

The **Pacific Dogwood**, *Cornus nuttallii* grows, often under Douglas Fir, from Vancouver Island and the parallel coast of BC, along the Coast Range to south CA and on the western flanks of the Cascade-Sierra Nevada to the San Gabriel Mountains, but is little seen in CA.

flw

fruits

flw

fruits

Flowering Dogwood

Pacific Dogwood

Madrones

The Heath family includes such diverse plants as heathers, rhododendrons and azaleas, and the madrones, all with similar flower structure. The Madrones are the biggest plants in the family, and the biggest of these is the Pacific Madrone.

The **Pacific Madrone**, *Arbutus menziesii* occasionally exceeds 100ft tall. Its shoots are stout, yellow-green for the first season, then bright orange and, as the bark thickens, deep red. The evergreen leaves are 2–6in long and blue-white beneath. Seedlings have finely toothed leaves. The flowers open in March in CA and in May in BC on erect, conical panicles, 8in long. The ½in fruit are green until most of them turn through orange to scarlet by October, but even in the south some of them are still green at that time. This tree is native from the southern half of Vancouver Island and the corresponding coast of BC along the coast and hills to south of Los Angeles, CA with small populations on Shasta and the Sierra Nevada.

The **Arizona Madrone**, *Arbutus arizonica* is a smaller tree, up to 50ft tall, with thinner slender leaves. It grows at 6000–8000ft in south AZ and southwest NM.

Pacific Madrone

Arizona Madrone

flws

fruits

Pacific Madrone

bark

Persimmons & Sourwood

The **Common Persimmon**, *Diospyros virginiana* is native over a wide area of the east, from NJ to the tip of FL and from the southern parts of PA to TX and the Gulf Coast. It is most common forming miles of hedges of small trees in AR and OK. The female flowers are on different trees from the male and are solitary, but the fruits are so numerous that they appear to hang in bunches, conspicuous and pale orange in late summer as the hanging leaves turn blackish green.

The **Sourwood**, *Oxydendron arboreum* has gray bark with thick, interwoven ridges and a high-domed, flat crown on sinuous branches. The undersides of its finely toothed leaves are smooth gray-green with white midribs. The fruits are ivory-colored like the flowers, and are hard to distinguish from late flowers amongst the scarlet leaves of fall. It is native from south PA, MD and DE to near New Orleans, LA but not near the coast. It is planted northwards in OH, NY and MA.

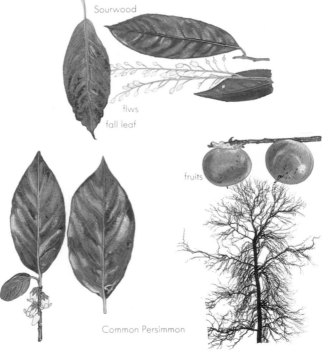

Sourwood

flws

fall leaf

fruits

Common Persimmon

Crapemyrtle & Russian Olive

The **Crapemyrtle**, *Lagerstroemia indica* is in the Loosestrife family, Lythraceae, and comes from China and Korea. It is an upright, bushy little tree which grows on several stems. It has pretty bark, smoothly ribbed, pink and gray in color, flecked green and with bald pink areas. The leaves are opposite, alternate or in threes. It has a long flowering season, bearing flowers which are as often white, pink or scarlet in the selected forms grown more in the far south, as the normal purplish red. It is common round the Coastal Plain from PA and DE to TX and north in the Mississippi Valley to Cairo, IL. It is occasionally seen in towns in CA in the west, particularly around Los Angeles.

The **Russian Olive**, *Elaeagnus angustifolia* is an oleaster, not an olive, from western Asia, very resistant to heat, drought and cold, and valued for planting in the middle west and southwestern regions, along roads, in shelterbelts and among factories. It is common from Winnipeg, MB, ND and SD, around Chicago, IL and through the prairies to NM and AZ and west in MT, UT and CO and in the dry interiors of BC and WA. It is much less planted east and south of Chicago.

Crapemyrtle flws

flws

Crapemyrtle

Russian Olive

Ash Trees

Of about 70 species of **Ash** in the world, 16 are native to North America, three of these extending over huge areas east to west and two with very wide north-south spans.

The **White Ash,** *Fraxinus americana* is one of these last, growing from Cape Breton Island and NS broadly to WI and mid-TX; it is a common woodland, park and city tree over most of that area. White Ash has male and female flowers on separate trees; towards the end of summer the leaves turn pale yellow, then orange before becoming a distinctive bronzy purple.

The **Black Ash,** *Fraxinus nigra* is a largely northern tree growing from NFD to Winnipeg, MB and south to IA, WV and NJ, not a large tree but planted in streets in northern cities. The terminal leaflet extends very narrowly down its stalk, the leaflet undersides are greener than in White Ash and fall color is pale yellow.

The **Green Ash,** *Fraxinus pennsylvanica* ranges from NS to around Lake Winnipeg into AB and south to the Gulf Coast in east TX. It is planted in streets west of this, in MT, ID, WY, CO, UT, NM, AZ and WA.

The **Blue Ash,** *Fraxinus quadrangulata*, is named from its four-angled young shoots growing four gray wings before shedding them in the fifth year and for the blue dye made from the inner bark. It has quite small, bright green leaves which turn pale yellow in fall. Its relatively small range occupies a rough arc from east TN through west OH and mid-IL to MO.

The **Velvet Ash,** *Fraxinus velutina* is a small slender tree with small 6in leaves and, typically with velvety hairs on the shoots, leafstalks and leaves. However it is very variable and some trees have no hairs. It extends from Mexico into west TX across much of

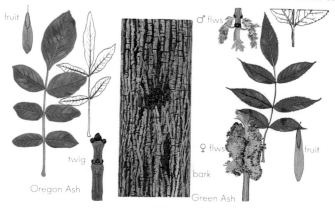

fruit

♂ flws

twig

♀ flws

bark

fruit

Oregon Ash

Green Ash

NM and AZ, looping through south UT and south NV into southern CA. It is planted in streets in these states.

The **Oregon Ash**, *Fraxinus latifolia* is native to bottomlands from the border north of Seattle, WA down the Coast Range to the Bay Area and along the flanks of the Sierra Nevada. It has unusually large leaves, often over a foot long, with broad, almost stalkless leaflets.

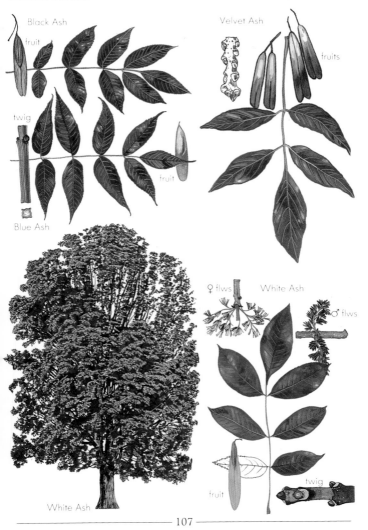

Black Ash

fruit

twig

Blue Ash

Velvet Ash

fruits

fruit

♀ flws   White Ash

♂ flws

fruit

twig

White Ash

Catalpas and others

The **Southern Catalpa**, *Catalpa bignonioides*, is in the Bignonia family, with the Trumpet Vine and is one of 11 species of *Catalpa* growing in N. America, the West Indies and China. With its close relative, the Northern Catalpa, it is found, apparently wild, in many parts of North America. However its original natural range was mainly in the southern parts of MS and AL near the coast, to the Gulf Coast of GA and FA. It is common today in hedges and parks from LA and TX to PA and OH, OK and AR, overlapping in the north with the Northern Catalpa. In the west it is found in WA, CO, NM, and occasionally in BC and CA. Big trees grow over 50ft tall but are often decrepit. The Golden Catalpa 'Aurea' is slower in growth, more tender and susceptible to sunscorch.

The **Northern Catalpa**, *Catalpa speciosa* makes a much taller, tougher tree than its southern relative, distinguished by its stature and by its long-tapered drip-tip leaves. The two can also be distinguished by their bark; that of the Southern Catalpa is orange-brown or dull pink-brown, scaly and crumbling in patches and not ridged while that of Northern Catalpa is dark gray and coarsely ridged. Its native range lies around the Mississippi and Ohio rivers in IL, IN, MO, AR and KY where it is very common in hedges, parks and gardens. It is common in BC and WA and along the coast in OR.

The **Royal Paulownia**, *Paulownia tomentosa* is related to the catalpas. It grows very fast, making in its second or third year from seed, a thick shoot to 8ft long with 18in stalks bearing leaves 18in

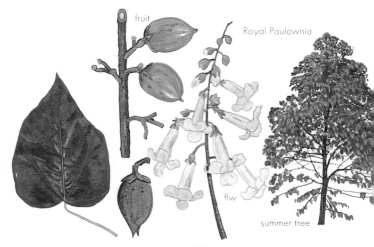

fruit

Royal Paulownia

flw

summer tree

long. It soon becomes fragile and liable to lose big branches; big trees grow up to 50ft tall. From ON to New England and NY it is found only in parks but from there south it is common.

The **Peppertree**, *Schinus molle*, from Brazil and Peru has taken over much of south Mexico and is grown in southern CA and TX. The hanging 8in leaves with 15–20 leaflets, on hanging shoots to 30ft long, and hanging slender 1ft bunches of dark pink or red fruits like currants, are very distinctive.

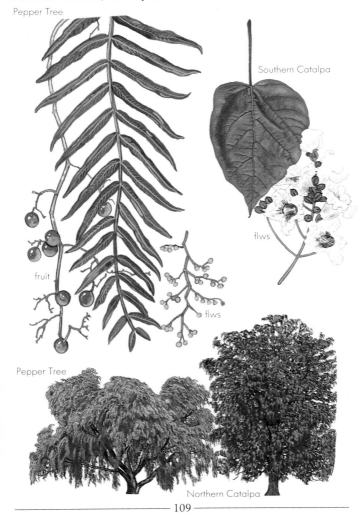

Pepper Tree

Southern Catalpa

flws

fruit

flws

Pepper Tree

Northern Catalpa

Yuccas & Palms

Yuccas or Spanish Bayonets are in the Agave family. They mostly have large multiple crowns near the ground, eventually forming a close group of stout short stems. They are confined to hot, sandy or rocky places. The Joshua Tree, *Yucca brevifolia* is more like a tree and grows up to 35ft tall. It begins to flower when about 10ft tall, its big ovoid flowerbud unfolding a stout 10in long spike, and its short, upturned branches begin at this height. These trees grow in the Mojave desert from southwest UT to CA and AZ.

Palms belong to the family Palmae. They are not true trees, having no wood in their trunks but instead their trunks are formed by internal growth around each leaf trace. In both yuccas and palms the leaves are large and evergreen and flower parts are in threes.

The **Cabbage Palmetto**, *Sabal palmetto* is native by the coast from Cape Hatteras, NC to south FL but has been widely planted and is common in streets and parks near the coast into TX, and inland in towns in NC, GA, AL, AZ, CA and NV. It usually grows 10 – 20ft tall; left to itself the trunk is covered with interlacing leaf bases with 1ft stubs, but in streets this is often cleaned down to smooth, gray bark. The 6ft orange flower panicles open in June.

The **California Washingtonia**, *Washingtonia filifera* is native from Palm Springs to the Mexican border but has been planted in more northern areas of CA also. The thick cluster of dead fan-leaves on the stem below the crown is typical of Washingtonias.

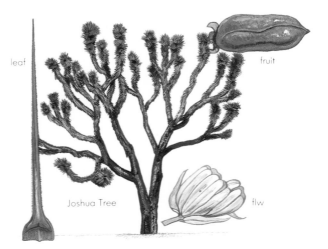

leaf

fruit

Joshua Tree

flw

The leaves are 6ft long on spine-edged 5ft stems and each is cut into 40 – 70 slender lobes. Panicles of yellow flowers, 10ft long, persist dead on the tree.

The **Canary Palm**, *Phoenix canariensis* is the most majestic and imposing of all palms outside the tropics. The leaves are 15 – 20ft long, 6ft across at the base and tapered evenly to the tips, and are made up of about 200 leaflets. Flower panicles emerge continually and are 3 – 5ft long, remaining dead on the tree for a long time. These trees are most common on the Gulf and CA coasts.

Cabbage Palmetto

leaf

Canary Palm

Cabbage Palmetto

fruit

leaf

Canary Palm

California Washingtonia

CONIFERS

Ginkgo & Podocarps

The **Ginkgo**, *Ginkgo biloba* or Maidenhair Tree is the odd tree out in this book, as it is in any book of plants, as it is neither a broadleafed tree nor a conifer. It is a ginkgo, and the only one left of a whole order of plants which were the dominant tree-forms worldwide 150 million years ago. Its leaves are unlike any other, with a broad close fan of radiating veins. They are shed in winter, first turning bright gold and then orange before falling.

The trees vary widely in shape, tending to be slender in hot dry areas but with dense hemispheric crowns of long rising branches in cool, wetter areas. Ginkgos are planted widely as street trees; from Montreal to New Orleans it is a downtown tree and the taller and closer the skyscrapers the more it dominates. In Manhattan there are places where only the Ginkgo and the Honey Locust seem able to survive. Male and female flowers are on separate trees. Female trees are usually loaded with fruit and this makes their use in streets undesirable, for the fruits not only rot into a messy pulp but rot with a foul smell.

The **Sentry Ginkgo** is much more restricted in distribution and outside NY and PA is quite scarce. It is a male form selected for its neat, narrow crown and can be raised from cuttings. In Philadelphia it is quite common.

The **Podocarps** (or Yellowwoods) are a large and widespread family of primitive conifers, highly unusual in ranging from New Zealand to Japan in the southern hemisphere. There are many species of them grown in the streets of the Bay Area and San Diego and *Podocarpus nagi* from Japan is one of them. The Bigleaf Podocarp, *Podocarpus macrophyllus*, also from Japan, is commonly grown against buildings or clipped as a hedge from Sacramento to CA. It is the common podocarp in SC, LA, in Phoenix, AZ and in southern CA.

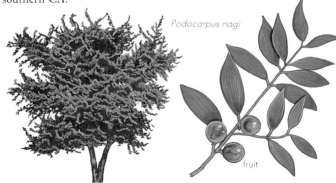

Podocarpus nagi

fruit

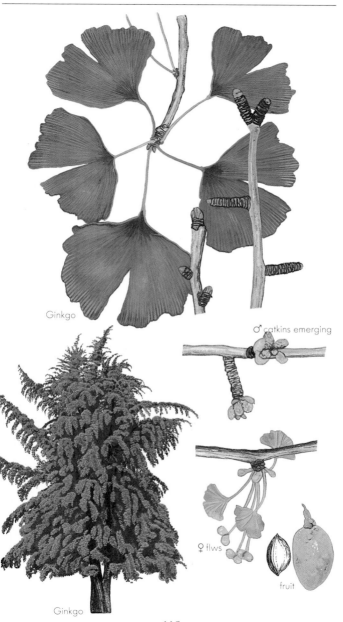

Ginkgo

♂ catkins emerging

♀ flws

fruit

Ginkgo

Yews

The **Yews** are the only widespread trees in a very primitive order of conifers separated from the others, together with the Torreyas and Cow-tail Pines. There are ten yews across the northern temperate regions, several being low shrubs. The trees tolerate heavier shade than almost any other and the most scanty soil among rocks, but must be in a moist place. They grow very slowly at first, then so slowly that growth is almost imperceptible. The timber is very hard and strong, and durable, and old trees are often hollow, held together by the hard wood. All parts of the tree, except the edible sweet red flesh of the 'berry' contain a powerful poisonous alkaloid, taxine, including the large seed.

The **Canada Yew**, *Taxus canadensis* is really only a shrub, growing up to 5ft tall, and found from NF to MB and TN. It is the only yew with male and female flowers on the same tree.

The **Pacific Yew**, *Taxus brevifolia* grows in the shade in damp woods from around Prince Rupert, BC and AK in a broad belt along the Pacific slopes to mid-CA in the Sierra Nevada and in another from interior south BC to MT and ID. In the interior it forms a shrub but in coastal BC, WA and OR it can exceed 50ft.

The **English Yew**, *Taxus baccata* grows from southern Scandinavia to North Africa and is the biggest of the yews, the oldest being up to 90ft tall and 30ft around. This yew is planted in towns and gardens and often clipped into a hedge from Montreal, PQ through New England, NY and PA to DC and west through OH and IL to WI, and more rarely south to TN.

The **Irish Yew** is a female form of the English Yew with the leaves in whorls around vertical shoots. It is very scarce in the east

bark

Pacific Yew

fruit

but a common town and garden plant in the west, from BC and OR to CA, becoming less frequent in the south.

The **Japanese Yew**, *Taxus cuspidata* is hardier than the English Yew, but is little seen north of NY or west of Chicago; there are many in NJ and PA. It makes a broad low tree and has golden-tawny color on the underside of the abruptly short-spined leaves. These are more raised and stiffer than those of the English Yew.

English Yew

♀ flws

♂ flws

Japanese Yew

fruit

English Yew

Irish Yew

Torreyas & Monkey-puzzles

The **Torreyas** are in the same family as the yews. There are five species, one in California, another in FL and GA, two in China and one in Japan. In Torreyas, the fleshy aril growing up around the seed, which in yews is thick, scarlet and forms a deep cup, is thin, encloses the seed completely and ripens dark purple. The trees have an oily, sage-like scent.

The **California Torreya**, *Torreya californica* is found in two separated areas, one near the coast from Mendocino to the Santa Cruz mountains, in little canyons running down to the sea, and the other along the lower foothills of the Sierra Nevada from Eldorado to Tulare Counties.

The **Araucarias** or Monkey-puzzles are a southern hemisphere group of trees. They have whorled branches on stout, nearly cylindrical boles and hard leaves, often spine-tipped, large and leathery, or small and scale-like. The cones are large, spiny and normally on separate trees from the thick, drooping male catkins.

The **Monkey-puzzle**, *Araucaria araucana* comes from the Andes. It is the hardiest of the family but in North America it is barely hardy in the northeast. Further south the summers are too hot, but it is well suited to the west coast where it is common in BC and coastal WA, becoming less frequent through OR to CA.

The **Bunya-Bunya Pine**, *Araucaria bidwilli* and the **Norfolk Island Pine**, *Araucaria heterophylla* are both grown in mid and southern CA and in FL.

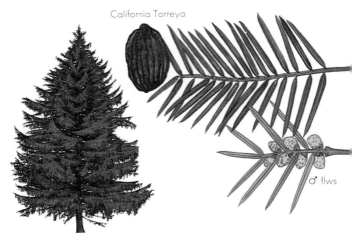

California Torreya

♂ flws

♂ flws

♀ flw

Monkey-puzzle

shoot

cone

Monkey-puzzle

Norfolk Island Pine

seedling

juvenile foliage

Norfolk Island Pine

Cypresses

The **Cypresses** are of two general kinds, 'true cypresses' and 'false cypresses'. Trees in the genus *Cupressus*, the true cypresses, occur in Europe and North America; they have have big cones and small shoots making bunches. False cypresses, with small cones and foliage in flattened sprays, are found only in North America and eastern Asia. They belong to the genus, *Chamaecyparis*.

The **Monterey Cypress**, *Cupressus macrocarpa*, grows wild only on two low cliffs, one each side of Carmel, CA. In the southern grove the trees are bizarre in shape, with long slender branches at flat angles, densely covered in foliage. Trees planted south through Big Sur and Lucia hold such branches vertically. Yet this area the trees planted in other parts of CA are of more conventional shapes.

The **Alaska-cedar** is a false cypress, *Chamaecyparis nootkatensis*. The tree has a regular conic crown and hard thick foliage which is hanging and dark, relieved only in winter and spring by an abundance of pale yellow male flowers. Crushed foliage has an oily turpentine scent. The tree is native from Anchorage along the coast and islands to Puget Sound in BC, in the Olympic Mountains and Cascades of WA and OR south to the Siskiyou Mountains of northern CA. It is planted in many northern collections in the east.

The **Port Orford Cedar**, *Chamaecyparis lawsoniana*, is a native tree, once found from Coos Bay OR, along the coast to Mad River, CA and inland in the Klamath and Siskiyou mountains. Fires and

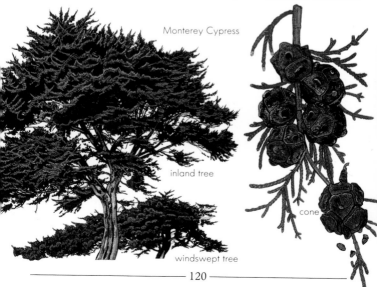

Monterey Cypress

inland tree

cone

windswept tree

logging have reduced its occurrence to scattered old timber and larger areas of second growth. Trees are planted and common in WA, BC and northern CA.

In the wild the trees have a uniform shape and are dark yellowish green; the crushed foliage has a resinous parsley scent. In Europe, many different forms of the Port Orford cedar have been produced, so that now over 250 named, distinct forms are in cultivation, with more added every year. They vary in shape from dwarf to medium and big trees, in color from blue to gold, gray and green, and in form and foliage from spreading and pendulous to upright and tufted. In N. America these cultivated forms are most common in BC, WA and northern CA.

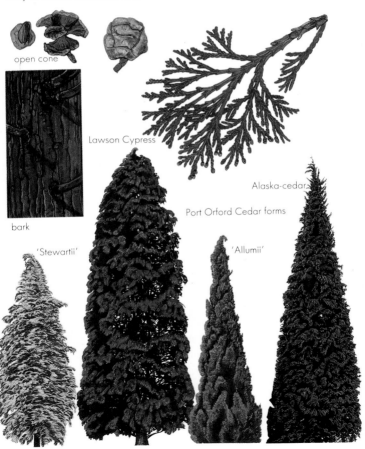

open cone

Lawson Cypress

bark

Alaska-cedar

Port Orford Cedar forms

'Stewartii'

'Allumii'

Junipers

The **Common Juniper**, *Juniperus communis* is the most widespread tree species in the world, and its low scrubby forms range the furthest north. It grows from Alaska, Greenland and Iceland across Europe and Asia to the Bering Sea and south in North America to the Olympic Mountains, Sierra Nevada, AZ and NM and in the east to NC. In N. America it is a low shrub, except in a few locations in the east, where it can be 15ft tall.

The **Eastern Redcedar**, *Juniperus virginiana* is the common juniper of the eastern half of N. America, colonizing roadside banks and old fields from ME to TX and SD. The bark peels in thin brown strips from the deeply fluted trunk. Spiny juvenile leaves radiate from the ends of weak shoots of adult scale foliage, and from the bases of stronger shoots. Female trees may be blue-white in summer from the little bloomed fruits.

The **Rocky Mountain Juniper**, *Juniperus scopulorum* takes over westward where the Eastern Redcedar leaves off. The two are very similar but there is a wide gap between their ranges east of the Rocky Mountains, so location is the key. Further west it is common and grown in towns from AB to WA, WY and CO.

The **Western Juniper**, *Juniperus occidentalis* is frequent from WA to the southern cross-ranges, CA on dry hillsides usually as a slender tree growing under Ponderosa Pine. In some places, however it forms huge low trees. The crushed foliage has a scent of sage and turpentine.

The **Utah Juniper**, *Juniperus osteosperma* is seen for miles as candelabra-shaped trees, none above 20ft tall, in the deserts from WY and UT to CA and AZ around the Grand Canyon. It has bark in gray-brown strips and thick rounded foliage.

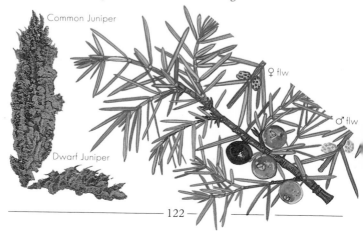

Common Juniper

♀ flw

♂ flw

Dwarf Juniper

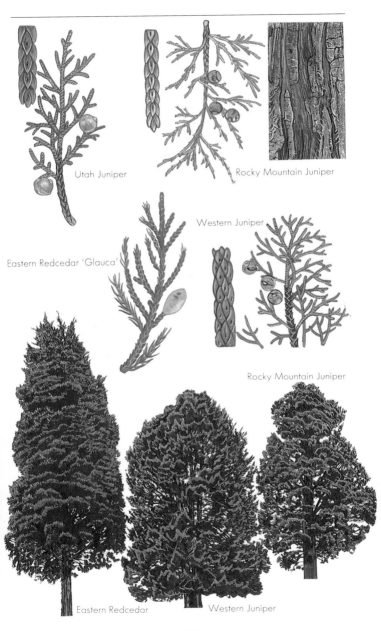

Utah Juniper

Rocky Mountain Juniper

Eastern Redcedar 'Glauca'

Western Juniper

Rocky Mountain Juniper

Eastern Redcedar

Western Juniper

Arbor-vitae

The **Arbor-vitae** or Thujas are members of a small genus divided between North America and eastern Asia. They are in the cypress family, related most closely to the Incense Cedar, and similarly resinous and aromatic. Their timber is light, strong and very durable.

The **Northern White Cedar**, *Thuja occidentalis* is a small and not very long-lived tree of swampy ground from the mouth of the St Lawrence River to SK, south round Lake Michigan to NY and in the Alleghenies to TN. Its leaves are pale yellow-green on the underside, have a raised gland on the upper side of each scale leaf and a scent of apple when crushed. The branches leave the stem more or less level and soon turn sharply upwards. It is planted in gardens in the northeast.

The **Western Redcedar**, *Thuja plicata* was long used by the Indians for canoes, houses, utensils and totem-poles. The timber is light, quite strong, but soft and easy to work and has a remarkable resistance to decay in water. Since it splits evenly it is also ideal for shingles, needing no paint and 80% of shingles used are of this thuja. It grows from AK along the coast and western slopes to CA and on the eastern ranges from AB to ID and MT. In the east it is common in Newport, RI and it is grown in large gardens in ON and NY. Big trees grow over 150ft tall.

The Golden-barred Thuja, '**Zebrina**' was raised in England around 1900 and is seen in the west only, commonly in BC and less so in WA.

The **Oriental Arborvitae**, *Thuja orientalis* has its foliage in

cone

bark

Oriental Arbor-vitae

erect flat sprays which are the same color on both sides. It has only the faintest vague scent when crushed. The cones have large, hooked beaks on about four of the scales and are bloomed blue-white in the summer and as it produces cones freely this is often its main feature. It is common each side of the front door in gardens, as well as in cemeteries and small town parks, on the Coastal Plain from MD to TX and west through NM and AZ to CA and NV.

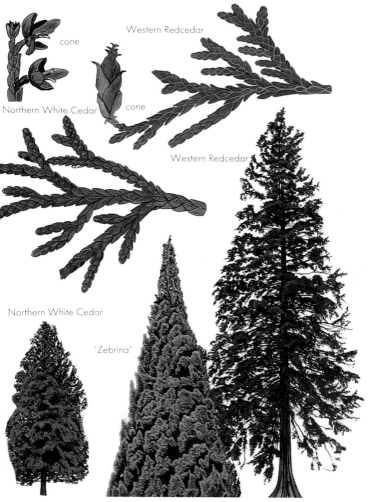

cone

Western Redcedar

Northern White Cedar

cone

Western Redcedar

Northern White Cedar

'Zebrina'

Giant Sequoia & Redwood

North America has two redwoods in the west and two bald-cypresses in the east, remnants of the once worldwide Redwood family. The **Giant Sequoia**, *Sequoiadendron giganteum* is today wild only in the western foothills of the southern half of the Sierra Nevada, CA in 72 groves; many of them have fewer than 20 adult trees but all are now fully protected. The Giant Sequoia is not quite the tallest, biggest in bole nor oldest tree in the world, but it is the biggest in volume of timber, with 'General Sherman' the champion, and is amongst the oldest, 'Grizzly Giant' being estimated to be over 3500 years.

It is now known that recurrent fire is necessary for the growth of the groves. It takes about 25 years of growth of brush and young trees after a fire in the groves, before there is enough fuel to sustain the next. The fires are started by lightning and burn briefly, the heat opening the cones, which remain for 30 years with live seeds inside. Seedlings grow in the ash-covered, cleared soil with White and Douglas Fir which outgrow the Sequoias but the next fire comes while their bark is still thin and resinous so they are mostly killed, leaving the thickly fibrous-barked Sequoias to grow on.

The **Redwood**, *Sequoia sempervirens* is the sea-fog tree of the hills a little back from the coast, from a few miles into OR south to beyond Big Sur, CA. In the high rainfall northern areas of this belt, trees over 300ft tall stand in close formation; around Weott there are big woods of trees around 350ft tall and still growing. South of the Bay Area where there is no summer rain, the trees are above 250ft only where the shape of the land holds the sea-fog of the morning. Then the big trees are much further apart.

'General Sherman'   'General Grant'   'Boole Tree'

Giant Sequoia

♂ flws

young cones

Coast Redwood

♂ flws

Giant Sequoia

mature cone

mature cone having
shed seed

Giant Sequoia

Coast Redwood

127

Baldcypress & Dawn Redwood

A few members of the Redwood family are deciduous, two are baldcypresses in eastern North America and two are in China.

The **Baldcypress**, *Taxodium distichum* is confined in the wild to swamps, flooding river-plains and the edges of tidal, brackish lagoons; in these places it grows pneumatophores or 'knees'. These arise from the roots at 60 or more feet from the tree, each a broad little pillar eventually 4–5ft tall, rather like termite mounds, with the typical bark of the tree trunk and with the top a dome rising from a recess inside a thick, rounded rim. It takes some 50 years for a tree to show knees, which contain spongy wood tissues and must help to provide the roots with oxygen. The species ranges from DE and the Pine Barrens of NJ and Dismal Swamp, VA along the coast and inland along river bottoms in NC, SC and GA, to around Orlando, FL. South of this it is replaced by the Pondcypress, but it continues along the plains into TX, through AR, along the Mississippi in MO and IL and along the Ohio in IN. It is also widely planted north of its range.

The **Pondcypress**, var. *nutans or Taxodium ascendens* at its most distinct has its new shoots rising vertically and appearing thread-like as the leaves are held closely to them. In the form 'Nutans' the shoots arch over from the ends of the branches, but trees intermediate between these and the Baldcypress can easily be found. The Pondcypress is wild from VA to eastern LA and is dominant in the Everglades and south FL generally.

Dawn Redwood

cone

The **Dawn Redwood**, *Metasequoia glyptostroboides* was only a well-known fossil until details of trees found in China in 1941 were published in 1945. Trees were planted in 1949–50 in big gardens and parks from ON and MA to Houston, TX and from BC to CA. Growth is exceptionally rapid, 25–30 year old trees being 75–80ft tall. It grows best on Long Island, NY and in DE and PA. The Dawn Redwood differs from the Baldcypress in the leaves and shoots being opposite, the crown more open and the leaves bigger, broader and unfolding some two months earlier.

Baldcypress

♂ catkin

cone

Pondcypress

Baldcypress

Silver Firs

The **Silver Firs**, *Abies* species, are about 40 very resinous, usually tall trees, with regular conic crowns and whorled branches. They grow all around the northern hemisphere. They differ from spruces in their leaves being leathery and rarely spined and in their female flowers and cones standing erect on the tree until they disintegrate. Also the leaves arise from sucker-like bases which go with them as they fall, leaving the shoots smooth. Spruce leaves arise from pegs molded at their bases into the shoot as ridges, the falling leaves snap off leaving the pegs behind and the shoots coarsely roughened.

The **Balsam Fir**, *Abies balsamea* is amongst the most resinous of all the silver firs, large blisters of resin persisting in the bark, and the foliage needs only slight bruising to yield its aromatic, balsam scent. This tree is the main source of Canada Balsam used for mounting microscope specimens. It grows from the coast of central Labrador to PA, across PQ to SK and northeast AB, south to IA, WI and MI.

The **White Fir**, *Abies concolor* is the eastern form of the much bigger Pacific White Fir. It grows in the eastern Rocky Mountains from ID to NM and AZ, and is the commonest western silver fir planted in the east. It has a regularly narrow conic crown with short level branches and its leaves are blue-green with gray-blue stripes. Big trees may grow 100ft tall.

The **Pacific White Fir**, var. *lowiana* grows from the Cascades of OR, through the Siskiyou Mountains and in the Coast Range to CA and all down the Sierra Nevada. It can form a superb and shapely tree, over 220ft tall.

Balsam Fir cone

Noble Fir bark

The **Noble Fir**, *Abies procera* stands out in the forest with its blue-gray foliage. In the wild it is restricted to the Cascades in WA and OR and to a few peaks in the Coast Range and Siskiyou Mountains. The majority of trees planted in eastern gardens are blue-white. It is apt to have a broken top because it lines the top shoots with big, heavy cones from fairly early in its life.

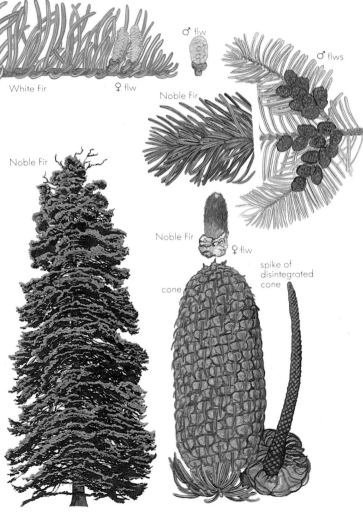

White Fir

♂ flw

♀ flw

♂ flws

Noble Fir

Noble Fir

Noble Fir

♀ flw

cone

spike of disintegrated cone

Silver Firs

The **Grand Fir**, *Abies grandis* was the tallest of all silver firs, once exceeding 300ft, although none today is as tall. The bruised foliage has a scent of oranges. Cones grow only on the top branches of trees over a hundred years old, 150 – 200ft above ground and disintegrate on the tree. It grows from the north of Vancouver Island and BC along the coast to mid-CA.

The **California Red Fir**, *Abies magnifica* ranges from the Cascade Mountains of mid-OR and the Siskiyou Mountains to the southern parts of the Sierra Nevada, CA. The trees grow above the 5000ft altitude line, mainly between 6000 and 8000ft and many superb specimens are seen in places popular with tourists. They grow up to 170 – 180ft tall. The name 'Red Fir' comes from the rich red bark of older trees at high elevations, but many others have nearly black bark, thickly ridged pale gray.

Wherever a road in the Rocky Mountains climbs a pass to 10,000ft, narrow spires of the **Subalpine Fir**, *Abies lasiocarpa* come into view. It ranges from Yukon, AB and UT to AZ and is a snowline tree, most slender where the snowfall is heaviest.

The **Pacific Silver Fir** or Beautiful Fir, *Abies amabilis* is another resinous fir like the Balsam Fir, with blisters on the bark, but only when young. The fragrance arising from bruised foliage is a citrus, fruity one like tangerines. Its main range is from the extreme south of AK to the Olympic Mountains, WA and inland along the Selkirk and Cascade Mountains to OR. It stands out among other tall silver firs for its narrow crown of blackish foliage on short level branches from a silvery stem. Big trees reach 150 – 200ft tall.

Pacific Silver Fir

cone

Subalpine Fir

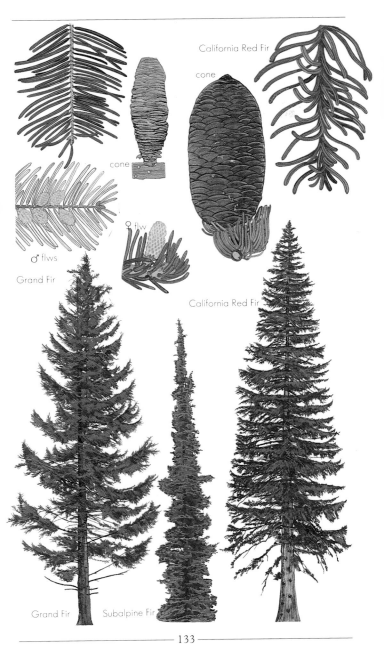

California Red Fir

cone

cone

♂ flws

♀ flw

Grand Fir

California Red Fir

Grand Fir   Subalpine Fir

Douglas Firs

The **Douglas Fir**, *Pseudotsuga menziesii* provides one of the main timbers of the world, being exceptionally good and strong for construction work. Vast stands of this tree in WA and OR carry more usable timber per acre than any other commercial stands except the Redwoods, and have created great wealth in those states. The tree grows from around Prince Rupert, BC, south along the coast to Monterey, CA and inland through southwest AB in mountains to MT and CO to NM and in the Sierra Nevada in CA.

The trees growing from the coasts to the western crests of the Rocky Mountains of the USA, known as the **Coastal Douglas Fir**, form some of the tallest and most magnificent woods in the world. In the valleys of Vancouver Island and in WA the world's tallest trees were growing until around 1900, several recorded as over 350ft tall and the Mineral Tree in WA as 385 – 395ft. Few of these remain now and the finest wood left is usually agreed to be a grove of trees near Quinault Lake, WA with top heights of 290 – 305ft.

The **Rocky Mountain Douglas Fir**, var. *glauca*, is the form that grows in the interior and on the eastern crests of the Rocky Mountains, at an altitude of 9500ft in many parts. It is a much smaller tree than the Coastal form, usually with rough black bark and variably bluish foliage. The leaves stand up more from the shoots and lack the strong, sweet fruity fragrance of the Coastal form while the copper-colored cones have long protruded bracts bent out level or curved downwards. The female flowers are usually bright crimson while those of the Coastal Douglas Fir tend to be greenish pink, rose pink, crimson, yellow, white or green.

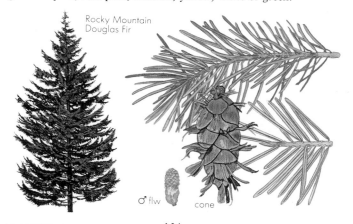

Rocky Mountain Douglas Fir

♂ flw   cone

The **Bigcone Douglas Fir**, *Pseudotsuga macrocarpa* is the only Douglas Fir with hard, spine-tipped leaves and cones up to 7in long, although usually around 5in long. The crown is broadly conical with sparse, long, nearly level branches and drooping foliage. It is found in CA in the cross-ranges at 1500 – 7000ft from the Santa Inez Mountains to the San Bernadino Mountains and on a few ranges south to the border and Baja California.

Bigcone Douglas Fir

♂ flws

♀ flws

Douglas Fir

immature Douglas Fir

Cedars

The **Cedars** are a group of four species in the genus *Cedrus* in the family Pinaceae; they are characterized by woody cones and are strictly an Old World group confined to the Mediterranean area and the Western Himalayas.

The **Cedar of Lebanon**, *Cedrus libani* grows in a small grove on Mount Lebanon, Syria, and on the Taurus and Anti-taurus Mountains in Turkey. It has been grown in Europe since 1638 when seed was brought to England. It is rare in North America and grows in a few large gardens from MA to OH and in BC and WA. It is a big spreading tree, up to 100ft or more tall, and has one or several trunks and branches which spread far and level, with the tips level or slightly drooping in old trees. The length of the needles, useful in separating cedars, is around 1in.

The **Atlas Cedar**, *Cedrus atlantica* from the Atlas Mountains in Algeria and Morocco, is almost always seen in one of the very gray-blue forms. The leaves are shorter than those of the Cedar of Lebanon, the bark much paler gray and the branches arise at an angle of about 45° with their tips at the same angle. It is common from MA along the Coastal Plain to GA, especially in RI. Inland it is scarce in ON and OH but frequent in PA and from KY to TN.

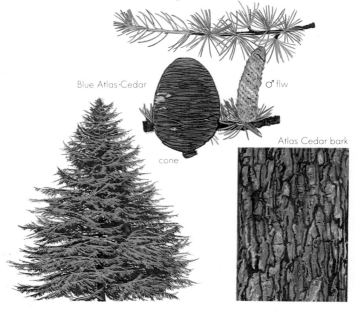

Blue Atlas-Cedar

♂ flw

cone

Atlas Cedar bark

The **Deodar Cedar**, *Cedrus deodara* has been reported to grow 250ft tall in the Punjab, in the middle of its range from Afghanistan along the Western Himalaya. It grows with a dropper leader, arching over at the tip, and usually maintains a single trunk through the conical crown. It has longer leaves than the other cedars, up to 1½in long, stout and deep green, although they may be dusty gray in the hot dry areas of CA. It is less hardy than the others, and is only common in the east from VA southwards along the Gulf Coast into TX and along the Mississippi Valley. It is also grown in the west, especially around Vancouver and in CA.

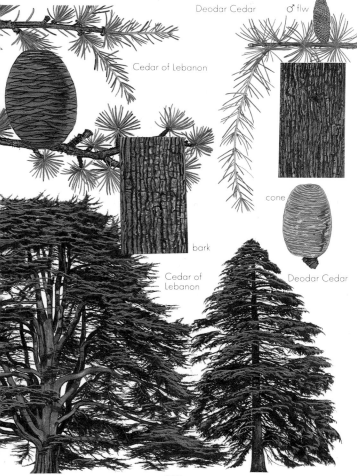

Deodar Cedar

♂ flw

Cedar of Lebanon

bark

cone

Cedar of Lebanon

Deodar Cedar

Larches

The **Larches** are deciduous conifers bearing woody cones ripening within the year. Larches' leaves are borne in the same way as in the cedars. A new shoot has spirally arranged single leaves and lateral buds; in the next year, the buds enlarge into short spurs bearing close whorls of 30 – 40 leaves. Before falling, the leaves turn luminous gold. Larches are pioneer trees, seeding out onto open land and they will not grow properly in shade. Fully grown trees must be well separated and plantations must be thinned regularly. There are ten species of larch, three in North America. One of these is a lowland species with a wide distribution and the other two are mountain trees with restricted distributions.

The **Tamarack**, *Larix laricina* grows from near the northern limit for trees, from Labrador to AK, south to northeastern BC and round the Great Lakes to PA and MD. Tamarack bark has no ridges but is finely flaking, dull pink or pink-brown. The flowers are very small, slender and bright red.

The **Western Larch**, *Larix occidentalis* is the biggest larch of all, up to 220ft tall. It grows at 2000 – 7000ft high from southeast BC into ID and MT and eastern WA and OR. Its leaves are bright grassy green and keeled beneath, and the bracts of the cones project as whiskers. Its bark soon becomes widely fissured into thick pink-brown scaly ridges. In BC it tends to be broadly conical with rising branches, but in the USA it has a narrow spire and level branches.

The **Subalpine Larch**, *Larix lyallii* is a timberline tree growing from 5000 – 8000ft on the southern end of the AB/BC border, on a few peaks in ID and MT and on the eastern flanks of the Cascades

Subalpine Larch

cones

Tamarack

in WA, everywhere within the range of the Western Larch but above it. It is like a short, stunted, rather weeping Western Larch.

The **European Larch**, *Larix decidua* from the Alps, is planted in gardens in the east and in plantations particularly in the Adirondacks. There are also trees in the west, especially in BC and WA.

♂ flws

♀ flws

cone

European Larch

European Larch

cone

Western Larch

Spruces

The **Spruces** consist of about 35 species distributed across the Northern Hemisphere in a pattern similar to that of the larches, with a few widely spread across the northern plains and most in small areas in the south. They have scaling, flaking but never ridged bark; harsh foliage with stiff, often spine-tipped leaves; and shoots roughened by pegs left when the leaves fall. Their cones are hanging, woody or leathery, ripening in the first year and shed complete; the female flowers are erect and bright red, the male flowers ovoid or globular, growing at various angles on upper shoots and strung around lower hanging shoots.

The most widespread and common spruce in North America is the exotic **Norway Spruce**, *Picea abies*, from the European Alps, Scandinavia and western Russia. In many areas on each side of the Canadian/US border it is used as a farm shelterbelt tree. Two main types of crown, 'brush' and 'comb' are seen mixed in these belts, the 'brush' with normal spruce, bunched shoots and the 'comb' with more sparse, upcurving branches from which the shoots hang in lines. It is common from Montreal, PQ south to Norfolk, VA and on the plains to NC, through MN, IN and IL to MO and south in the Mississippi Valley. It is common in BC and WA.

The **White Spruce**, *Picea glauca* is native in a broad band across the continent from Labrador and ME to AK south to MI, mid-SK, interior BC and MT. It is also planted in NY and OH, less frequently in PA, MD and DE. It has a remarkably slender crown in mountainous areas, but in the east older trees have domed tops. Crushed foliage emits a scent described as mousey.

♂ flws

♀ flw

cone

White Spruce

The **Serbian Spruce**, *Picea omorika*, from Yugoslavia, has flat needles, like spruces of the Pacific shores of America and Asia, and in contrast to other European and eastern Asian species which have needles which are almost square in cross section. It is seen, with its distinct spired crown, in parks and gardens from ON and MA through PA and OH to WI and MN, and around Vancouver and Victoria, in BC in the west.

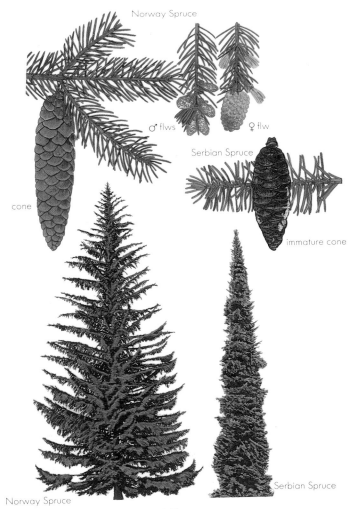

Norway Spruce

♂ flws   ♀ flw

Serbian Spruce

cone

immature cone

Norway Spruce

Serbian Spruce

Spruces

The **Sitka Spruce**, *Picea sitchensis* is the biggest spruce in the world and the fastest growing. In its native stands by the Pacific Coast it has been found growing over 300ft tall. It is also the spruce with the greatest north-south spread, from the Alaskan Kodiak Island and north to Anchorage, AK, on islands and mainland coast inlets and hillsides through BC, WA and OR to CA. The Sitka is one of the prickliest spruces, its stiff hard needles being sharply spined. Old trees have broadly columnar crowns of long, gently arched branches sparsely set with short, hanging shoots.

The **Engelmann Spruce**, *Picea engelmannii* also has a big north-south range, nearly as long but much broader and inland, from northern BC and AB on interior mountains to CO, NM and AZ and along the Cascades to the CA border. It is planted in roadside gardens and parks within its range. The leaves are soft or rather stiff but not rigid, and are short-spined. Crushed, they have a scent of menthol or camphor. The orange-brown ripe cones have scales with toothed margins.

The **Red Spruce**, *Picea rubens* grows, often in dense stands, from Cape Breton Island, NS through NB and ME to southern PQ and ON and southward and on mountain tops through NY, PA, VA and NC just into TN. With the Fraser Fir it clothes many of the highest peaks of the Blue Ridge Mountains, NC, to 6000ft. It can grow to 100ft tall. Typically the bright grassy green leaves stand nearly vertically slender, wiry and short, nearly round in section and when crushed they smell of apples or candlewax, but in

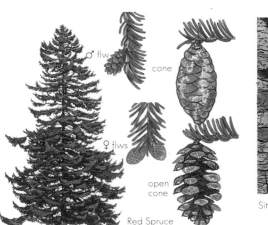

♂ flws

cone

♀ flws

open cone

Red Spruce

Sitka Spruce bark

parts of the north it has hybridized with the Black Spruce, and the needles are darker bluer green and more spreading. The crimson male flowers curve upwards as they shed pollen and the 2in cones ripen pale orange-brown, often in bunches. The bark is rich purple-brown or dark orange-brown, dark gray on older trees at high altitudes. It flakes finely until it fissures into small, concave plates. The crown is narrowly conic and dense, with lower branches bending down then sweeping upwards to the tips.

Sitka Spruce

♀ flw

cone

♂ flw

Englemann Spruce 'Glauca'

cone

Sitka Spruce

Engelmann Spruce

Spruces

The **Blue Spruce**, *Picea pungens* is variably blue-gray to dark blue-green in the wild, where it grows from 6000–11000ft in ID, UT, WY and CO to NM. It has been recorded growing up to 150ft tall. A particularly blue form, known as 'Glauca' or 'Koster's' is the commonest and most widely spread spruce grown in towns and gardens in North America. It is planted from Montreal, PQ through MB and AB into BC. It is also common in the Prairie states and in New England. The name '*pungens*' means 'sharp' and the rigid, stout leaves are well spined and stand up from the stout shoots, which in the blue forms can be orange or dark brown.

The **Black Spruce**, *Picea mariana* is native from northeastern PA across a vast area to Labrador and AK, through all Canada except BC, southern AB and SK. The crown is a dense mass of fine twigs and looks quite blue from a distance; in many areas it ages with a bushy, domed top but in the southern parts of its range in the Rocky Mountains it may be slender. Growth is always slow so the leading shoots on immature trees are short. The very small, slender, ½in leaves spread all round the pink-brown shoots and have a scent of menthol cough sweets when crushed. The numerous male flowers are small and crimson while the red females are crowded on the topmost branches. They are borne by young trees not yet 10ft tall and ripen into bunched, shiny red-brown cones less than 2in long.

Oriental Spruce

cone

♀ flws

♂ flws

Blue Spruce

cone

The **Oriental Spruce**, *Picea orientalis* is the only spruce with leaves even shorter than the Black Spruce. They are a quarter to a third of an inch long, deep glossy green on all four surfaces and with bevelled round tips. They lie closely all round young shoots and are parted beneath as they age, persisting for eight years or more. It has pale gray bark with dark freckles, darkening with age and cracking into regular small raised plates. The crown forms a narrow spire. This spruce, from the Caucasus Mountains and Turkey, is the most frequently planted in North America after the Norway Spruce. It is grown in northeastern parts from ON to OH.

Blue Spruce

♂ flws

♀ flws

Black Spruce

cone

Black Spruce

Hemlocks

The **Hemlocks** are close relatives of the spruces. They have small, slender leaves and, with one exception, very small, droplet-like cones borne freely over the densely foliaged crowns. There are four species in North America, two in the east and two in the west; and about eight in eastern Asia.

The finest and tallest by far is the **Western Hemlock**, *Tsuga heterophylla* whose range extends from AK along the coastal slopes and islands to northern CA, inland to the Cascade Mountains in OR and in an interior belt from the Selkirk Mountains, BC to MT and ID. It bears deep shade better than any other conifer when young, except the Redwoods sprouting from living stumps. In dense rain forests seedlings grow mainly on decaying logs. The hemlock has a 'dropper' leading shoot, on which the new vulnerable tip hangs a foot or two below the woody apex of the arch, which takes the knocks as it grows between overhead branches. The Western Hemlock makes an elegant slender tree with slightly up-curved branches and great quantities of hanging foliage. It can grow up to 4ft a year on damp soils and big trees grow over 200ft tall.

The **Eastern Hemlock**, *Tsuga canadensis* has tapering leaves growing in a line along and closely above each shoot, twisted to show the silver-banded undersides. On the northern plains it can be big and strongly branched but in the mountain valleys in the south the trees are more slender and conic. The range is from NS and NB across southern PQ and ON, south of Lake Superior to WI and MN, south to MD by the coast and south to GA and AL through

o⁷ flw

young cone

Eastern Hemlock

Mountain Hemlock

PA and OH. It is common in parks and gardens within this range. Big trees grow over 100ft tall.

The **Mountain Hemlock**, *Tsuga mertensiana* is almost a snowline tree from AK, on mountain tops along the coast and down the Rocky Mountains to BC, MT and CA. It is unlike most hemlocks in having large spruce-like cones and uniformly blue-gray or green leaves all around short spur-like shoots. The bark is orange-brown, thinly flaking and stripping vertically until it becomes hard and ridged, often dark gray with age.

Western Hemlock

young cone

♀ flw

♂ flws

open cone

Eastern Hemlock

Western Hemlock

Two-needle Pines

The **Pines** number about 110, of which 36 are native to North America. Pines are alone among conifers in having their leaves or needles united at the base into bundles in a sheath. These are short shoots split into two, three or five so the needles of a two-needle pine are semi-circular in cross-section and are thick and stiff, those in bundles of three are triangular and more slender and those in fives tend to be more slender still and often drooping; these are called Blue or White Pines. White Pines have easily worked timber and are called 'soft pines' while two and three needle pines are 'hard pines'. The pines on this page are all two-needle pines.

The **Shore Pine**, *Pinus contorta* is the coastal form of the Lodgepole Pine, found from AK to CA. It is usually a windblown bushy tree of small size. The Sierra Nevada form, var. *murrayana*, which grows from the Columbia River to the cross ranges is a fine tree, growing over 100ft tall.

The **Lodgepole Pine**, var. *latifolia* has longer, broader and paler yellowish leaves and ranges from central AK down the interior and eastern Rocky Mountains and the Black Hills, SD to Mexico. This is the pine of the Yellowstone Park geyser-basins and gorge. The prickly cones stay on the tree with seeds enclosed for decades until a fire comes through and the whole area is regenerated with trees of the same age.

The **Jack Pine**, *Pinus banksiana* holds its cones pointing outwards, the opposite to the Lodgepole which holds them pointing

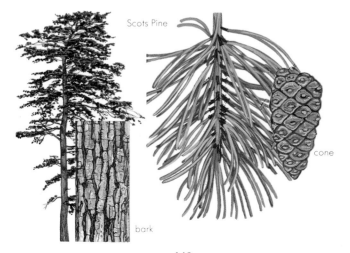

Scots Pine

cone

bark

inwards, and they stay closed until gray, lichened and grown into the bark, and fire is needed to spread the tree. It ranges from Cape Breton Island, NS to the Mackenzie River, NWT and to WI, MI and NH.

The **Scots Pine**, *Pinus sylvestris* with short twisted blue-gray leaves and dark red or pink bark is common in town and country from PQ to Norfolk, VA and from SK to AR and IA. There are also trees in UT, a few through OR and WA until it is common again in BC.

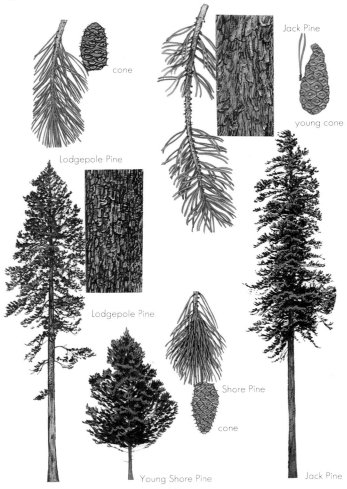

cone

Jack Pine

young cone

Lodgepole Pine

Lodgepole Pine

Shore Pine

cone

Young Shore Pine

Jack Pine

Three-needle Pines

The **Ponderosa Pine**, *Pinus ponderosa* or Western Yellow Pine is the dominant pine of the United States Rocky Mountains from the Canadian border to the Mexican border, both of which it crosses. Vast areas of the southwest, now semi-desert or scrub, were stands of this pine until cleared by logging, fire and over-grazing. Ponderosa Pine grows from near sea-level in WA to 10,000ft in AZ on any soil. The bark is gray pink to pink-brown in long plates, shedding 2in, irregularly lobed flakes like jigsaw puzzle pieces, which pile up around its base. The crown retains its neat conic shape, with a spire of upswept small side-branches above more level branching. It may grow 150−220ft tall. The cones are about 4−5in long, about half the size of those of the similar Jeffrey Pine, and, like them, have down-curved prickles on the scales.

The **Digger Pine**, *Pinus sabiniana* is the pine of the drier foothills around the Central Valley of CA where it has such peculiarly thin foliage that the woodland is almost transparent. The slender bloomed shoots are curved and bear thin, widely separated whorls of needles, 10−12in long. The stem divides low into several vertical trunks to make a tall dome often heavily clustered with the squat, 10in cones.

The **Knobcone Pine**, *Pinus attenuata* is immediately recognizable by its bright, grass-green foliage and upright branches with downward pointing gray cones. It grows in the foothills from south OR through northern CA.

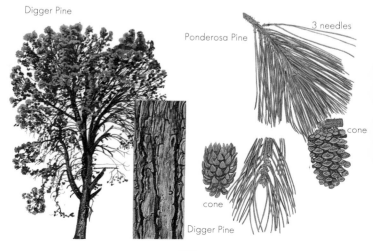

Digger Pine

Ponderosa Pine

3 needles

cone

cone

Digger Pine

The **Slash Pine**, *Pinus elliottii* has its 8–12in long needles in twos and threes; they are lemon-scented when crushed. It makes a broad columnar dark tree with a big cone of sinuous branches. It is native near the coast from SC to LA and replaces Loblolly and Longleaf Pines in southern FL.

The **Shortleaf Pine**, *Pinus echinata* also has its leaves mixed two or three in a bundle, but they are only 2–3in long. It has pink-gray or dark orange-gray, scaly, often shaggy bark and an open, broad columnar crown with many old cones. The branches bear many short, grassy sprouts, as in Pitch and Pond Pines. It is native from NY to IL south to east TX.

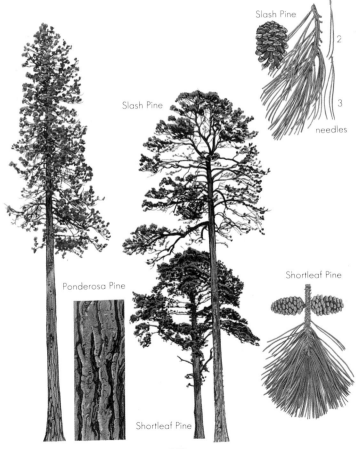

Slash Pine

Slash Pine

2

3

needles

Shortleaf Pine

Ponderosa Pine

Shortleaf Pine

Three-needle Pines

The **Monterey Pine**, *Pinus radiata* is one of the conifers that was migrating northwards again after the Ice Ages, close to the California coast and was trapped in little pockets of land when the coast eroded into islands and bays. The Monterey Pine and Gowen Cypress were caught on the Monterey peninsular, the Bishop Pine reached Big Lagoon; the Torrey Pine stuck at La Jolla. The main area of the Monterey Pine is a 6000 acre stand near Carmel with the Seventeen Mile Drive around it. The trees are 60−80ft tall and die young, infested by dwarf mistletoe. The tree does not like its native areas. It is planted in shelterbelts in Central Valley and south to San Diego. This is a three-needle pine with soft, slender needles, bright green at close quarters but nearly black on distant trees.

The **Pitch Pine**, *Pinus rigida*, another three-needle pine, has thick, stiff needles only 4in long in the main crown. But it grows great numbers of short sprouts and these have needles 5in long on white shoots. The trunk and main branches can be densely covered in this hanging foliage. It is common in mountains from NY to GA.

The **Loblolly Pine**, *Pinus taeda* is the common tall roadside plantation pine on the plains from VA to east TX, and into AR, NJ and FL. It has slender red-brown or pinkish shoots and the needles are slender, 6−7in long and in threes. The 4−5in long cones have short stalks and sharp spreading spines.

The **Pinyon Pines** are a small group of bushy little trees bearing large cones with few scales and big, edible seeds. They extend from Mexico into southwestern USA. The Mexican Pinyon Pine, *Pinus cembroides* grows near the border and has needles in threes. The

Monterey Pine

bark

3 needles

cone

Pinyon Pine, *Pinus edulis* has hard, thick, curved 2in needles mostly in pairs. This is the little pine which grows on dry hills in AZ and NM, north to CO and UT. The Parry Pinyon, *Pinus quadrifolia* has needles in fours; it is rare and grows in the mountains of south CA. The Singleleaf Pinyon, *Pinus monophylla* has its needles fused into a single, rigid, sharp spine. It ranges north to the Wasatch Mountains, UT and across the interior ranges in NV to the Sierra Nevada, CA and Mexico.

Pitch Pine

Loblolly Pine

cone

Pinyon Pine

cone

3 needles

cone

cone

seeds

Pitch Pine

Pinyon Pine

Five-needle Pines

The **Sugar Pine**, *Pinus lambertiana* is the largest of all the world's pines and grows the largest cones, 15 – 24in long, 2in across when green and 4in when woody and open. The bark is usually orange-pink, finely fissured into small regular, smoothly rounded scales. It is reputed to have been known 300ft tall but today few are known over 220ft. The range is from the Cascades of mid-OR, along the Sierra Nevada to the cross ranges; through the Siskiyous to the Coast Ranges to Sonoma County and again in the Santa Lucia Mountains.

The **Western White Pine**, *Pinus monticola* grows in the eastern Rocky Mountains from AB and BC to ID and MT and on the western coast and hills from BC and WA south in the mountains to the Sierra Nevada, CA. Young trees are slender and upswept. Old trees are also slender with short level branches, often conical tips and clean, cylindrical trunks clad in smooth, regular, rounded scales of shiny brown, black or red-brown.

The **Eastern White Pine**, *Pinus strobus* is the only 5 – needle pine east of the Rocky Mountains and was the biggest tree there and the most important timber-tree in all America in the last century. From NF to MN and IA it grows in large pure stands and south along the Allegheny Mountains to TN and GA it becomes more scattered among hardwood and hemlock forests. This tree is frequently planted in the west, in small gardens in BC and WA.

The **Bristlecone Pine**, *Pinus aristata* is found, in the typical form, with leaves heavily white-speckled with resin, high in the dry

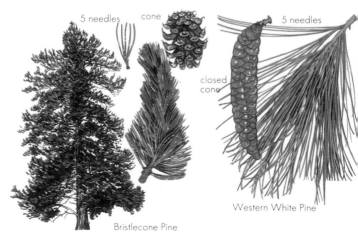

5 needles   cone

closed cone

5 needles

Western White Pine

Bristlecone Pine

mountains of CO and NM. It is a 'foxtail' pine, in which the 1½in long leaves, in fives, are pressed rather near the shoots making them look like ropes. The Intermountain Bristlecone Pine, var. *longaeva* lacks the white spots, has shorter spines on the cones and a sweet resin scent instead of smelling like turpentine. It grows on the White and Inyo Mountains in CA and on the highest ranges in NV and UT. It is amongst these trees that the oldest trees in the world are found, up to 5000 years old.

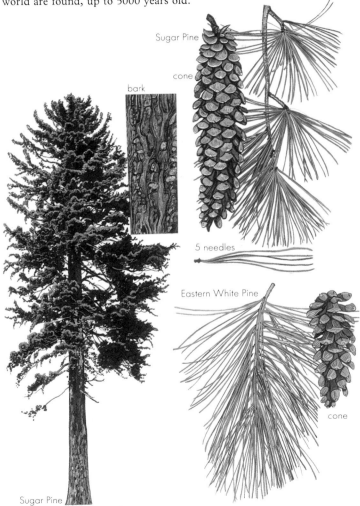

Sugar Pine

cone

bark

5 needles

Eastern White Pine

cone

Sugar Pine

PRACTICAL REFERENCE SECTION

A concise guide to the practicalities of
the selection and cultivation of trees

Suitable Trees for the Garden

Given here is a list of particularly good trees to plant for the garden, with an indication of the type of climate they need. Where no climatic needs are given, the tree is tolerant of considerable heat, cold and drought. If planted in an arid zone, it will only thrive under irrigation.

Key

F	Few and light frosts	**T**	Temperate, general
FF	No frosts	**TC**	Temperate, cool
H	Hot summers	**TW**	Temperate, warm
	R	Rainy; no long dry summer	

Common Name	Climate	Good Features
Alder		
Italian	**TR**	Robust grower, fine foliage and early catkins
Apple		
'Charlottae'	**T**	Flowers and fruit
'Dorothea'	**T**	Flowers and fruit
Hupeh crab	**T**	Flowers and fruit, strong growth
Pillar	**T**	Neat upright shape; fall color
Ash		
Caucasian	**T**	Fine foliage; fall color; robust
Basswood		
American	**TR**	Fine foliage; good shape
Beech		
American	**TR**	Foliage, bark, fall color
'Dawyck'	**TR**	Shape; fall color
Birch		
Swedish	**T**	Weeping, deeply cut foliage; bark
Buckeye		
Yellow	**TR**	Foliage; fall color
Catalpa		
Hybrid	**T**	Vigor; big foliage and flowerheads
Cherry		
Sato	**TC**	Flowers, fall color

Crape Myrtle	**FH**	Flowers, bark

Chestnut		
Japanese Horse	**TR**	Foliage, flowers, fall color
Indian	**TR**	Foliage, late flowers

Cypress		
Arizona Smooth	**T**	Shape, color
Cripp's Golden	**TR**	Shape, color
Leyland	**TR**	Extreme vigor

Dogwood		
Flowering	**T**	Flowers, fruit, fall color, bark

Dovetree	**TR**	Flowers

Elm		
Chinese		Foliage, bark, resistance to disease

Fir		
Bristlecone	**TR**	Foliage, shape, cone
Californian silver	**TR**	Vigor, foliage, shape
Caucasian	**TR**	Foliage, shape
Douglas	**TR**	Foliage, vigor
Nikko	**TR**	Foliage, shape, good near cities
Noble	**TR**	Blue-gray foliage, cone
White	**TR**	Blue-gray foliage, esp. 'Violacea'

Ginkgo		Foliage, fall color, shape, interest

Goldenrain tree		
Formosan	**FH**	Flowers, fruit, foliage

Hazel		
Turkish	**T**	Early catkins, vigor, shape; good in cities

Hemlock		
Carolina	**TR**	Foliage
Western	**TR**	Vigor, shape

Honeylocust		
'Sunburst'		Color, tolerance

Hornbeam		
Pyramidal	**TR**	Shape, fall color

Katsura	TR	Foliage, fall color, shape
Keaki	T	Foliage, fall color

Larch

European	R	Early foliage, fall color, vigor

Linden

Silver	TR	Robust in cities, foliage, scent
Silver pendent	TR	Robust in cities, foliage, scent

Madrone	TR	Bark, foliage, flowers, fruit

Maple

Amur		Tolerance cold and heat, foliage
Oregon	TR	Foliage, flowers, fall color
Paperbark	TR	Bark, fall color
Snakebarks	TR	(Several species.) Bark, foliage, fall color
Trident	T	Foliage, fall color

Oak

Black	TR	Foliage, fall color
Chinkapin	HR	Foliage
Cypress	TR	Shape
Pin	R	Vigor, foliage, fall color
Scarlet	R	Foliage, fall color
Shingle	R	Foliage

Parasol tree	HR	Foliage

Pear

Bradford		Shape, fall color
Chanticleer		Shape, fall color

Pine

Bhutan	TR	Foliage, vigor, cones
Bishop		Resistance to sea wind
Canary	H	Shape, foliage
Japanese Black		Resistance to sea wind
Jeffrey	TR	Shape, tolerance, cones
Slash	HF	Foliage, vigor
Torrey	HF	Foliage, vigor

Poplar
    Bolle's   Shape, foliage
    Lombardy   Shape, fall color

Poplar		
Bolle's		Shape, foliage
Lombardy		Shape, fall color
Redwood		
Dawn	**R**	Foliage, shape, vigor
Spruce		
Brewer	**TR**	Shape
Colorado Blue	**R**	Color
Oriental	**TR**	Shape
Serbian	**TR**	Narrow spire shape
Sitka	**TR**	Vigor, color, resists sea winds
Sweetgum		Foliage, fall color
Tupelo	**TR**	Foliage, fall color
Thorn		
Plumleaf	**T**	Foliage, fall color, toughness
Scarlet	**T**	Foliage, fruit
Washington		Foliage, fruit
Walnut		
Black	**TR**	Foliage, fall color, shape
Japanese	**TR**	Foliage, cold-resistance
Wingnut		
Caucasian	**TR**	Foliage, vigor, fall color
Hybrid	**TR**	Foliage, vigor, fruit

Planting a Tree

Preparing the Hole

Nearly all trees make more reliable, sturdy growth in their first few years if they are transplanted, than if seed is sown and the plants left undisturbed. Nevertheless it is a wholly unnatural break in its growth pattern for a tree to be planted – one to which it cannot have evolved a response – and the operation should be planned to cause the least possible disruption to growth. The crucial point is to make the move as early in the tree's life as possible, to allow it the formative first five or six years in its final position. The bigger and older a tree is when planted, the more its growth is retarded, the longer it takes to make the big root system it needs for growth and stability. A tree eight feet tall is easily crippled for life by being moved, and no tree so big should even be considered for purchase unless it has a big root system prepared over several years in the nursery.

The best size for planting is $1 - 1\frac{1}{2}$ft, from open ground or a large container, where the roots have never been cramped. Such a plant, with all its roots, planted firmly, is stable from the start, must not be staked and will grow rapidly to build a stout bole and shapely crown. A tall plant has already made its lower crown in response to conditions in the nursery lines, and so it will be drawn up with a slender, weak stem, often made worse by being tied to a stake. For a healthy plant, the stem must grow in the place where the tree is to spend its life and in response to the surroundings there. The foliage of a tree feeds its roots and the roots feed the foliage. A tree planted out usually has less shelter than in a nursery and its foliage is under more stress from drying winds. So it needs a vigorous root system. With the usual tiny, cramped incomplete one of a tall plant it can scarcely leaf out at all, much less make new shoots. So there are few leaves to feed the roots during their vital time for expansion into new soil. Thus, little growth can be made on the roots, and little on shoots; the tree is locked into a stage of minimum growth and has a dire struggle to survive, for many years.

A small plant with almost natural rooting evades this trap. Roots must be spread out to reach the new soil, not left in a ball. Pot-bound roots must be at least partially unravelled even if some break and need to be cut back. The size of hole needed can then be seen – big enough to take the spread roots with a small margin extra. The bottom of the hole is dug out to allow 6in of good soil or leaf mould beneath the tree, and the base well broken up if it is a heavy soil. A mixture of the surrounding soil, compost and sand is put round the spread roots and gently firmed.

In poor sandy soils a little superphosphate fertilizer spread over

Preparing the Hole

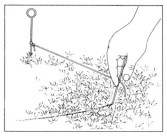

1. *A circular area of cleared ground is most suitable, and easily marked for the new tree. Swing a marker 3ft from a pin.*

2. *Remove a thin top layer of turf and put it aside. Most of the good topsoil stays to be dug out and mixed to make the backfill.*

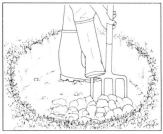

3. *Break up the bottom of the hole well, if it is compacted, to provide good drainage. If it is good loam, it can just be dug over.*

4. *Break up the turf taken from the top and put it at the bottom of the hole, where it will break down into good rooting soil.*

5. *Spread a layer of well-rotted manure, leaf mould or compost over the turves to conserve moisture and allow easy rooting.*

6. *Firm in the bottom layers before the tree roots are put in place, to ensure that there are no pockets of air in the lower layers.*

Planting the tree

1. *Hold the tree in position and shake it up and down gently, as soil is spread around and among the roots.*

2. *Using a cane to mark the soil level, hold the tree while filling the hole to old level and firming.*

3. *Tread the top firm; then lightly fork the surface to break it up slightly to allow in water and air.*

4. *Trees should be provided with a short stake to hold them still until the roots have grown.*

the bottom before placing the tree in the hole aids rapid root-growth; while some slow-release nitrogenous fertilizer like bonemeal added to the backfill improves early shoot growth.

The level of the surface on the stem before planting can be seen, and filling brings the new soil to the same place; then after heavy firming it is made good to that level again. In light soils the new tree and a 3ft radius around is left 4in below the surrounding level; the tree needs frequent watering and the water then stays around the tree.

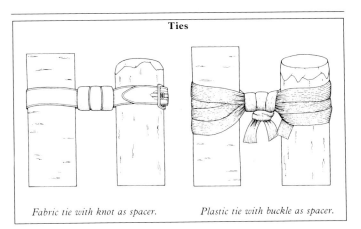

Ties

Fabric tie with knot as spacer.   *Plastic tie with buckle as spacer.*

Staking and Tying

Standard and other large trees need a stake, not to hold the stem up but just to hold it still until the new roots have grown. After that it is bad for the tree to be staked, as it needs to sway to grow its proper, stout stem. A short strong stake, firmly set 1ft away holds a tie on the bole 1ft away from the ground and is removed after the second growing season and the winter gales. A large tree from a container is best held by a triangle of three short stakes, because driving one into the root ball would very likely damage important roots. (One stake each side is adequate for trees of moderate size).

Stakes should not be longer than is needed to hold the ties at 1½ft. Projecting into the crown they can damage branches and serve no purpose, unless sometimes in public places, they lessen vandal damage. The heaviest standards with big tops may need their support at one third of the height of their stems.

Stakes should be long enough to allow them to be buried 1½ – 2ft deep, be knot-free and straight-grained for strength. They must be free from disease, preferably tanalized or otherwise treated with preservative unless they are Western Red Cedar.

Ties must have some elasticity to allow unhindered expansion of the stem even in the two seasons at most that they are needed. They must have spacers to prevent the stake rubbing the tree and be fixed firmly, on the stake to prevent them from, slipping down in bad weather.

Pruning and Shaping

Trees normally assume their best shape in their own way. Only those grown for their fruit need annual pruning to increase the size, number or accessibility of the fruit. In the case of all other trees, the term 'pruning' has a very different meaning, covering two separate operations.

The first of these is to aid the natural process of shedding the first, lowest branches in order to give a clean, smooth bole. In woodland these are soon shaded out and shed, but on single trees the strongest branches extend into the light and keep growing at their tips while the inner shoots and smaller branches become bare. Left alone, these make a tangle of dead wood hiding the bole and soon full of nettles and rubbish, while big low branches disfigure the tree. Even where a lawn-tree is intended to be feathered to the ground, the early removal of the branch tangle on the bottom 5ft allows the next layer to drop around a clean bole. Other trees can have 6ft of clean stem by the time they are 20ft tall.

The second operation – shaping – is required only to rectify a fault in growth. A forking leading shoot can be singled as soon as it is seen. A forked, two-stem tree is ugly and vulnerable to storms. Misplaced or over-vigorously protruding branches should be removed when necessary.

Where to cut

Removing side branches from a stem early in its life, when they are only a few inches in diameter, can be done at any time of year. The small scars which are left close in a year or two, leaving a smooth stem. Removing older stems and taking branches from the crown leaves big scars. Branches usually swell out at their origin to a conic protrusion. This causes conflict between two desired aims – a minimum size of scar and a cut flush with the major stem or branch to leave it smooth. Controversy raged for 400 years and decay followed pruning whether the cut was flush, left a marked stub or if a rough unreasoned compromise was made. Dr A. Shigo of New Hampshire has shown exactly where the cuts should be made and why.

The Shigo Method

In beech alone there was an old method of pruning small branches leaving a 2in stub. Coral-spot fungus was sure to infect this but by the time it reached the main stem, the tree had sealed off the scar and the stub would fall off with the fungus to leave a healed scar. Were the cut flush with the bole the fungus could have entered the stem and decayed a large, deep scar.

Dr Shigo has shown that *all* trees isolate areas of decay with barriers of resistant cells; that the junctions of branches have the tissues for growing the barriers already disposed in a pattern to prepare for natural shedding, and he has described how these show on the tree. A 'branch bark ridge' on the upper side and a 'branch collar' on the underside mark the outer rim of tissues that will grow the barrier, which is conical, pointing inwards.

The natural death of a branch causes the collar to enlarge. When the branch is decayed and breaks off it will tend to take with it the conical insertion. However if this remains and rots, it is isolated from the main stem, and the exterior is sealed in by growth from the enlarged collar. The cut must be close to but clear of the collar.

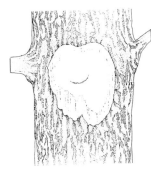

The Wrong Way *Cutting flush with the stem leaves a smooth surface, but the branch is thickest at the base so such a cut leaves a bigger scar. Worse, this cut removes the collar of tissues whose function is to heal the scar, so the wound heals slowly. Few dressings inhibit decay and many make a skin which cracks and lets water lodge against the scar. Unless repainted often, dressings thus encourage decay. The correct cut leaves the collar intact to close the scar.*

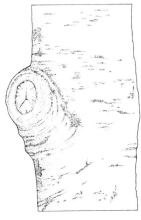

The Right Way *The correct cut is from just clear of the 'branch bark ridge' above to just clear of the collar below. The collar may not show; then the angle of the cut is shown by the* angle that the ridge makes away from the branch. The cut is at the same angle from the vertical in the opposite direction.

Singling a Fork

A symmetrical fork in new growth on a very young tree may be left until new growth begins next season

but no longer. Unequal forks may call for a choice between a weak shoot and a strong one that is more offset.

Singling Sprouts

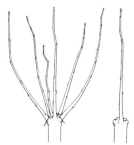 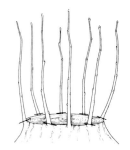

A eucalypt or similar tree may regrow after a hard frost as many shoots from ground level. Choose one strong shoot and cut the others.

A sprouting stump can be regrown as a tree, cutting out all but the single strongest and most shapely new shoot.

Crown Thinning

 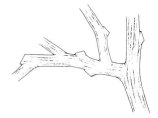

Some broadleaf trees have crowns which can become congested. Savage cutting makes them worse.

Thinning the crown by intelligent removal of excess leafage on whole branch systems, always cutting back to a main branch, cures the trouble.

Cutting	**Cleaning the Bole**
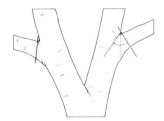	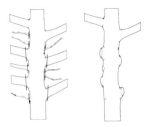
All but the lightest branches are cut to a stub before pruning, to prevent tearing. First a shallow undercut, then the full cut a few inches outside.	*A bole can be cleaned when branches are 4–6in across. Beyond that it would leave too much scar. A clean bole for 5ft is a minimum aim.*

Improving Growth of Young Trees

Trees are sociable plants and in nature they normally arise and grow in groups, either of their own species only or amongst others. Even the pioneer species – the first to colonize bare ground – usually spring up in numbers together.

The new bare sites are largely those cleared by fire (due to lightning before the arrival of man and often afterwards also) but greatly increased by deliberate burning to clear the land for grazing and crops. In western North America most of the coniferous forests have large areas of uniform age which can be dated back to a fire and most of the trees have a life-cycle adapted to the average period between fires, which itself is fixed by the time needed for enough combustible material to accumulate. Other new sites arise on a smaller scale from landslides, rivers changing course and swamps drying out. Pioneer species have light seeds, often with fluff or wings, and are carried by the wind much further than heavier fruits which are dispersed by mammals or birds, usually in established woods. The trees bearing the heavier fruits therefore come in only after the pioneers have created a form of woodland. Hence the successor species are also adapted to growing up among trees – at first those of a different species from themselves.

The aspens, poplars and willows have fluff on their seeds and are long distance pioneers. The birches with minute winged seeds can travel a fair distance, and pines, with heavy winged seeds, are usually short distance pioneers.

The first trees on new land grow in conditions very different

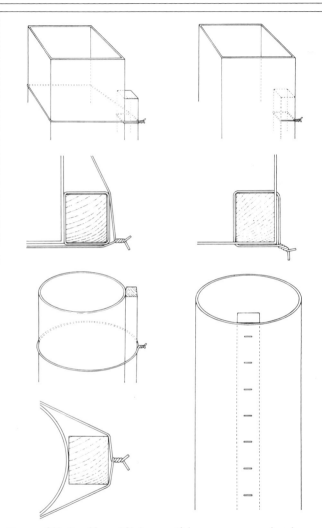

Types of Shelter *Normal Shelters are 4ft long, square or round, and can be translucent, green or brown. They last 5 years, until degraded by sunlight. Weeds must be removed before setting up the shelter; those outside may be sprayed. Shelters must be held firmly and the base pushed into the soil. A tile batten 1in² is driven 1ft into loam, 20in into sand, 1in from the stem. Galvanised mild steel wire of 16 gauge can be used to hold the shelter to the batten. If the batten is softwood, staples may be used.*

from those found in woodlands. There will be open sky and either newly formed soil or newly burned surfaces. If new, the soil will usually be short of the nutrients needed for growth, particularly in nitrogen, and lacking entirely in humus. If burned, it will also lack nitrogen but be high in potash, and the top at least will lack humus. So pioneer species need to adapt to poor, often open, sandy soils and to have a low demand for nutrients. But the overwhelming factor on new exposed sites is the wind which causes the soil, at best open and poor in humus, to dry out rapidly. Pioneer trees must be able to withstand drought. They can do so by early development of wide, deep roots and by having small or thick-skinned leaves.

Small tough leaves or dense hairs on shoots and leaves lessen the damaging drying effect of the wind on the foliage. Big thin leaves can be grown only by trees whose entire life is spent in the shelter of old woods. The pioneer trees have no need of dense foliage to catch enough light, since they grow in open places. Their leaves work only in nearly full light, and are shed when they become shaded by others and the crowns remain light and open. This allows the wind to filter through where a dense crown would be damaged by strong gusts. It also allows strong growth of the early arrivals among the ground herbs, and later the growth of the more shade-bearing trees that will take over when the pioneers have created shelter and their leaf fall has built up a much improved soil.

The pioneers make rapid early growth, flower and fruit within a few years of germinating from seed and tend to be short-lived. These qualities are further adaptations to their life-style. They do need, however, to modify the severity of their surroundings in order to grow well, or, in the more extreme sites, to grow at all. This can be done only by growing in large numbers together from the start, which is the normal result of seeding on to bare ground. Each tree then benefits from the shelter of the others and this common shelter increases as the trees grow and improves greatly the microclimate within the stand. Even the trees on the periphery benefit, since the trees behind retard the wind that sweeps through them. Height growth increases with distance from the edge.

The pioneer stands are usually fairly open, but there are exceptions such as the Aspen tracts following heath fires and the Lodgepole Pine stands in the interior Rocky Mountains, which arise and largely remain in very dense groups, despite a high rate of suppression and death.

Successor species are adapted to starting life in the sheltered, relatively humid conditions of woodlands, in a humus-rich, reasonably fertile soil. Many need open sky above them after varying periods and achieve this end either by outgrowing the species around them or by biding their time until the canopies above them fail and fall with age.

The conclusions to be drawn from all these factors is that a tree,

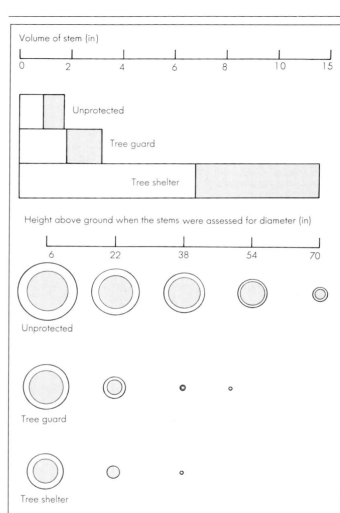

Volume of stem (in)

0   2   4   6   8   10   15

Unprotected

Tree guard

Tree shelter

Height above ground when the stems were assessed for diameter (in)

6   22   38   54   70

Unprotected

Tree guard

Tree shelter

Growth Comparisons: 3 and 4 years Oak. *60 trees. 20 control (unprotected); 20 with tree-guard (plastic net); and 20 with tree-shelter.*
TOP. *Volume of stems. Unshaded portion; third year: shaded portion; fourth year.*
BOTTOM. *The same trees, mean cross-sections at 16in intervals up the stems. Inner disc; size after 3 years; outer ring, growth in fourth year. Trees in shelters increase in stem volume in their third year as much as those in tree guards had increased in their four years from the acorn. Silver Birch, Norway Maple, Sycamore etc reacted similarly.*

of any kind, either planted singly or widely spaced on an open site as in most amenity plantings in parks or around buildings, faces conditions from which its natural manner of growth largely shields it. To make matters worse, it is usually planted out when it is far too big, and has spent too many years in the very different conditions of the nursery. The worst aspect for the tree is the sudden subjection to exposure.

Tuley Tubes
Graham Tuley of Great Britain experimented with translucent plastic 'tree shelters' of different materials, widths and heights. A narrow shelter gives a 'greenhouse effect', retaining within it the heat it receives from radiated light — an effect that is apparent if you put your hand into one on a cool day. In the calm damp warmth the side shoots grow big leaves which promote growth in the stem and leading shoot. They are short and congested but are removed when the stem is cleaned up. The shelter also protects the tree from damage by animals. Growth in many broadleaf trees is given a rapid early start, most spectacularly in oaks but all species tested have benefited when provided with shelters. Among conifers, only Japanese Larch responds strongly. Some trees, notably oaks, cannot hold up the big crown that results. They must be secured to the stake that held the shelter when the plastic has degraded away after the expected five years. Over 500,000 Tuley tubes were used in one year in Great Britain.

Measuring Height

The height of a tree less than about 20ft tall can be measured
accurately with a rod. The height of a tall tree can also be measured
reasonably closely but exact measurement of its height is normally
impracticable. Even climbing the tree can rarely solve the problem.
The path for the tape down the bole cannot be direct, the precise
tip cannot be seen by the climber or judged accurately, and the tree
may lean.

Height is reckoned from the highest point of the crown and this
may be, in an old many-headed conifer or a broad domed broadleaf
tree, many feet from the central axis. Its position has to be decided
from a distance and the point directly beneath it estimated from
under the crown. The bottom of a tree is the highest point to which
soil reaches up the bole. This prevents the extended bole and roots
on the downhill side of a steep slope from counting in the height.

Having observed the points between which the measurement is to
be made, the next thing to decide is the place from which to make
it. Accuracy is best at a distance from the tree which is equal to its
height and from the same level as its base. A rough estimate of the
height of the tree – 60, 90 or 120ft – is made and a position found
at about the equivalent distance as nearly level with the base as
possible, from which the top and bottom can be seen. A leaning
tree is sighted at a right-angle to the direction of the lean if
possible.

Measuring the height of a tree.

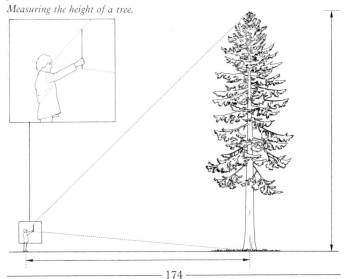

Estimating Age

The height and spread of a tree both increase with age until senility begins and then they decrease again. Both fail as indicators of age beyond the early years. Diameter and bole circumference increase every year of life, a ring of new wood being added annually. The circumference, measured at 5ft, is a good guide to age.

For big-growing trees (not those like apples and holly) the broad rule 'one inch per year' (roughly 2.5cm) increase in circumference applies regardless of species, region or altitude, over a wide span of years. Most trees add well over an inch a year in youth and gradually decline first to one inch and then to less. In an old tree the increase is on or close to one inch per year over a very long period. Wood added depends on the amount of foliage, so a tree crowded in a wood or having lost branches adds less each year and may fit 'one inch every two years'. A fully crowned oak 20ft around will usually be about 250 years old.

There are, however, both hares and tortoises among trees. Fast growth, that is three to four inches a year, is made each year by the best eucalypts, willows and poplars, also by Giant Sequoias, Coast Redwoods, Dawn Redwoods and some Grand Firs.

A few trees grow more than one inch a year for less than 100 years and then slow down. Examples are Scots Pine, Norway Spruce, Planeleaf Maple and European Linden. Approximate age for these trees when their circumference is more than 100 inches, is 100 years plus an extra year for every extra ½inch.

Gilbert White recorded the Selborne Yew to be 23ft round at 3ft up in 1789. In 1984 it was 25ft 7 in (7.8m) at the same point. This would make it about 1200 years old in White's day, 1400 years old today.

Range Maps

The historic ranges of native species are shown by solid shading. Those ranges extended by further planting of native species or the introduction of exotic species are marked by cross-shading. While large-scale maps give detail, as scale decreases small areas have to be combined in larger blocks. The small scale of the maps here cannot indicate how ranges have been fragmented by clearance, neither can they show how some trees are always confined to small areas such as river-bottomland or scattered hillsides. In exotic species, main areas of planting and naturalized seeding can be plotted from observation. While areas within which trees are scattered in gardens can be broadly marked, isolated planting in botanic gardens, like some in Denver, Colorado but seen elsewhere no nearer than Missouri or California, cannot be marked.

Black Willow *Named from the bark which is a useful feature in winter and in summer. Rarely planted but common within its natural range in or beside swampy bottomlands and the tallest willow there, usually with three or four stems.*

 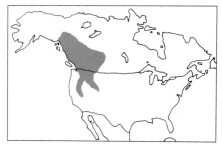

Mackenzie Willow *Usually seen as bushy, low roadside trees or many-stemmed bushes. Grown in some small gardens in Canada and cut back regularly partly for the bright orange bark of the long young shoots.*

 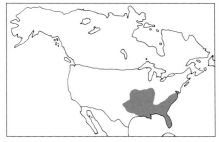

Coastal Plain Willow *A low, rounded bushy little tree on the margins of swampy bottomlands, in front of tall Black Willows. Distinctively yellow-green in leaf, it has dark gray, scaly and ridged bark. The leaves are up to 4in long.*

 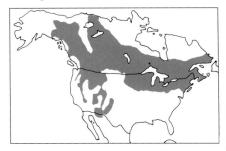

Quaking Aspen *Prominent in the Rocky Mountains, as roadside thickets of white stems, especially in CO and WY. Less striking bark and growth over much of the extensive eastern range, but equally spectacular bright gold foliage in fall.*

 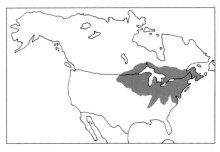

Bigtooth Aspen *The leaves may be 6in x 5in and are firm and solid. They are a fresh bright green and make this a handsome tree, although a short-lived one achieving no great size. The bark is very smooth, gray-green.*

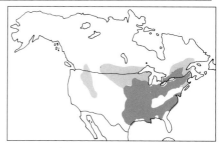

Eastern Cottonwood *As a young tree, slender and conic with branches in whorls; very open. Broadly domed, dense and leafy with age and reaching a great size. Quite bare of foliage when the catkins open in March at branch-tips.*

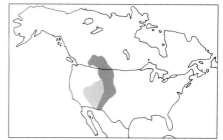

Plains Cottonwood *Much planted in the Prairie States for shade. The leaves are drawn out to long, entire tips and big branches bend down then sweep up with dense brushes of foliage, brilliant gold in fall.*

Black Cottonwood *A tall and often untidy, upright-branched tree, vulnerable to wind damage near the top. The heavy leaves are dark above but show white-painted undersides. The large buds are very resinous and fragrant when opening.*

 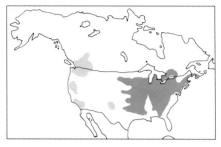

Black Walnut *A fine tree with large, bright green foliage. The crown of old trees is gaunt with a few large level, twisting branches high on a long, clear stem, all with nearly black bark with deep, complex ridging.*

Pecan *A fine tree, not unlike the Black Walnut, but the bark is scaly gray and becomes whiter with age. Hardy little beyond Washington DC, it has been planted extensively south of there, far beyond its assumed natural range.*

Mockernut Hickory *A hickory with smoother bark than most and heavy dark foliage which hangs in summer. The shoots have a covering of dense, fine but dark hairs, prominent also on the swollen bases of the leafstalks.*

Paper Birch *A highly variable tree across its great range. It has warty shoots, hairy leafstalks and few veins for the large size of each leaf. The bark is usually very white but in parts of the range it is orange or tends to dark purple.*

 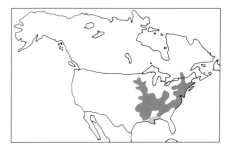

River Birch *The only birch with lobed leaves or silvered leaf undersides, this tree is common beside watercourses in the east, but is not confined to them. It may be a many-stemmed shrub but is often a single-boled tree of good size.*

 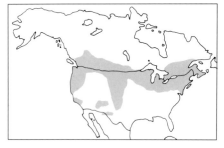

European White Birch *Planted widely in North America, it differs from native birches in the slender, pendulous outer shoots and in the diamond-shaped black patches on the bark. The warted shoots bear coarsely toothed rather small leaves.*

Red Alder *Confined to the damp woods of the lower hills of the Pacific slopes, this has the largest leaves and fruit of any native alder. The leaf margins are minutely rolled down. The bark is clearest white mid-range, in Oregon.*

 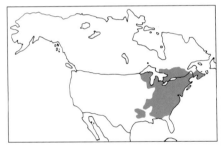

American Beech *In eastern woods in winter, the pale silvery bark and persisting bleached cream leaves give a ghostly aspect to the tree many trees have brushes of thin sprouts around the base.*

Tanoak *The only representative of this large group of oaks outside China, it grows in the far west, in the Coast Range and in the Sierra Nevada. The leaves last for four years, unfolding with brown woolly hairs beneath, soon blue-white.*

White Oak *Some fine old specimens have huge low branches although in woods the crown is mainly upright. Patches of shallow, finely plated bark often come away leaving paler areas. The upper leaves are deeply cut into curved lobes.*

Oregon White Oak *A broad-crowned tree with stout low branches. It has dense hairs on the shoots and the undersides of the leaves, and dark gray bark. In the fall the leaves are muddy dark brown.*

 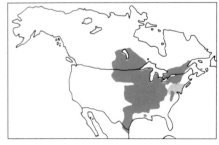

Bur Oak *This tree can grow the biggest acorns of any American oak, to 2in long in cups 2in across, with large protruding scales. In the midwest it ranges far to the north of the other oaks.*

Valley Oak *This tree covers miles of low, dry hill-country near the coast and in the Sierra foothills in southern CA, with few other trees. It has wide, spreading, twisting big branches and a broadly domed crown.*

Blackjack Oak *Plainly a red oak from the whisker-tipped lobes on the leaves and the acorns taking two years to ripen, this tree has quite different leaves from the others. The very broad, shallow and rounded lobes are distinct.*

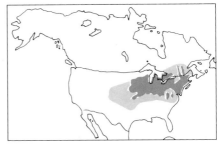

Pin Oak *The shapely growth of this tree, with a clean stem and regular, slender branches makes it popular for city streets. The underside of each leaf has large tufts of pale brown hairs in the main vein-angles.*

Emory Oak *This is a small tree of dry rocky and sandy sides of gulches and canyons around AZ. Its evergreen little two-inch leaves are hard, firm, dark green above and bright gray-green beneath with pale brown hairs.*

 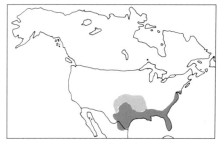

Live Oak *This is the tree whose arching branches spread widely, draped with Spanish Moss, to shade the approaches to the old plantation houses in SC. The hard, dark, evergreen leaves vary greatly in shape.*

 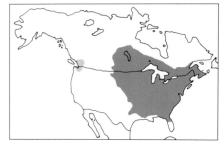

American Elm *Much the largest and most planted native elm, this is, despite losses from disease, still common in Main Street. Typically it has a broad dome, held high on big branches. Brownish red flowers are produced in early spring.*

Cedar Elm *In the southwestern interior states this is a common small roadside tree with upright shoots, remarkable for the leaves being so stiffly held that they do not move as the shoots are blown around. Fall colors are gray.*

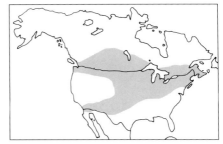

Siberian Elm *Native to the same regions as Elm Disease, this tree has a natural resistance to it and is widely planted for shade in the prairie regions, and frequently in other parts. It has widely arched branches.*

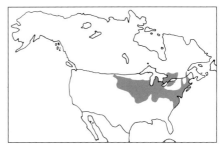

Hackberry *Hackberries have leaves with bases prominently three-nerved and margins entire or toothed or both. This one has the largest leaves, toothed on the outer half, sometimes on one side only. The bark has dark lumps and ridges.*

Sugarberry *This is in effect the hackberry of the southeast, with smaller leaves often not toothed at all. It is hardy when planted north to NY. It is quite a big street-tree in many southeastern cities.*

 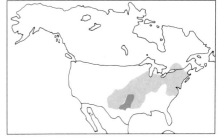

Osage Orange *A spined tree much planted long ago as hedges as far from its native Texas as PA and DE where there are the biggest old trees in parks and gardens. The female tree bears hard, heavy 4in globular fruit.*

 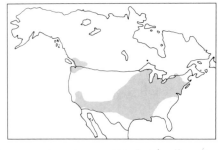

White Mulberry *A Chinese tree planted very widely but fragile so it becomes a large bush of stems from a broken hulk of bole. The fruits turn pink then ripen red, not purple or dark blackish red as in other mulberries.*

Yellow-poplar *A tree in the Magnolia family with similar flowers but very different, broadly lobe-ended leaves. The dark brown shallowly ridged bark is often on splendid trunks which may be 60ft high without a branch.*

 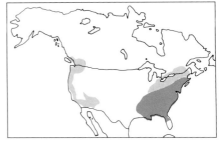

Sweetgum *The handsome starlike leaves of this tree emit a sweet scent when torn and turn gold, orange and scarlet, often mottled, in the fall. An eastern tree, it is much planted in the west.*

Sassafras *The leaves of this tree may have a lobe on one side, on both or none at all. Crushed, they give a vanilla and orange scent. In the fall, they turn fiery red. The bark is very dark and ridged.*

California Laurel *The leaves of this evergreen tree from the west coast emit a powerful spicy scent which can easily cause a sharp headache. It is usually seen as a number of stems with one base, but can form a single trunk 150ft tall.*

 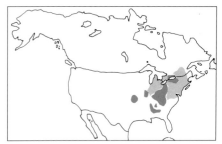

Cucumbertree *This magnolia often has a good straight trunk and is the only one with rich brown, narrowly ridged bark. It ranges further north and reaches greater size than the others. The undersides of the leaves have soft, fine hairs.*

 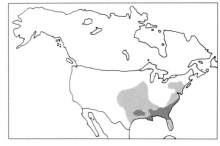

Southern Magnolia *Planted well to the north of its natural range, 40–50ft tall in PA gardens and in town streets in AR, it is often twice as tall on the Gulf Coast. The open flowers are strongly fragrant.*

Sycamore *This is often seen standing out in the woods by eastern streams, with its tall crown of branches and white bark mottled blue and orange. The ball-like fruits grow singly on 5in stems and measure 1½in across.*

California Sycamore *A smaller and less striking tree than the eastern Sycamore with five 1in fruits on each stalk. The leaves are hairy beneath and each is deeply cut into five lobes, either entire or with peg-like teeth.*

 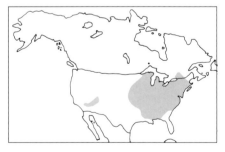

Bradford Pear *A seedling selected in Maryland from a Chinese species, this shapely tree is widely planted in streets and precincts. The white flowers begin to open in March before the leaves, from red-tipped buds.*

 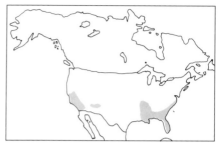

Loquat *The big, dark-wrinkled leaves of this Japanese fruit-tree are evergreen and grow on low, wide-branched trees. They are only seen south from Charleston SC in an arc round to the Bay Area, CA.*

Black Cherry *This tree is small in lowlands but tall, to over 100ft, in high valleys in the Great Smoky Mountains. It ranges widely across North America in one form or another from Nova Scotia to Guatemala.*

 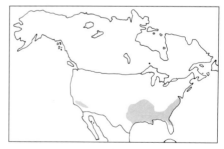

Chinaberry *Domed bushes of this Chinese tree are common in the deep south each side of the door or gate of little houses. There are a few tall trees in city squares. The doubly compound, dark green leaves tend to hang.*

American Holly *A dark evergreen, usually shapely tree, this is valued in PA and DE where summers are too hot for European Holly to be grown. The female trees bear rather small red berries through the winter until spring.*

 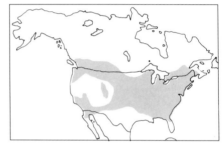

Tree of Heaven *A very vigorous, strongly suckering tree from north China, this spreads also by its many seeds, and has invaded inner suburbs of many cities in the warmer parts. Its big many-leaflet leaves unfold late and red.*

 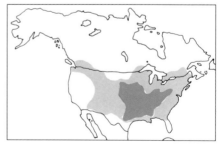

Honeylocust *From its extensive eastern range, this tree has been planted west and north in almost all city centers as it can grow well where few other trees can, in sidewalks among skyscrapers. It has brief pale gold fall colors.*

 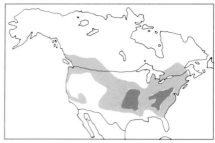

Black Locust *From a small eastern and central range, this tree has been planted far and wide and spreads by spiny suckers and seeds. It is late to unfold its leaves and early to shed them.*

 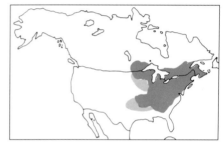

Sugar Maple *The fall colors of this tree are unexcelled in mixed fiery orange and scarlet, then brilliant red. The crown is usually tall-ovoid. The lobes of many leaves narrow towards their bases. The fruits are shed by midsummer.*

 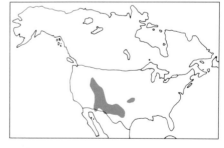

Canyon Maple *This is one of several species which are divergent forms of the Sugar Maple, and grows much further south and west than any other. Its small leaves turn orange in the fall.*

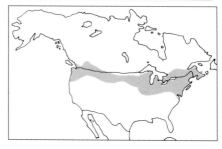

Norway Maple *Often planted among Sugar Maples, this tree has pale brown, finely ridged bark. The teeth on the leaves are finely whiskered and bunches of bright yellow flowers open before the leaves. It turns yellow and orange in fall.*

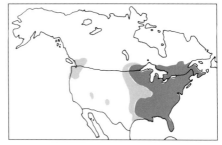

Red Maple *In early spring these trees stand out in woods, parks and gardens with all the shoots wreathed in flowers. They range in color from bright red to somewhat brownish red, and give the tree its name.*

Striped Maple *The only snakebark maple not confined to eastern Asia. The large broad leaves, very shallowly three-lobed, are rich green until turning pale yellow and falling early. The flowers are like slender, paired catkins.*

Boxelder *This is unique among maples in its leaves, in some forms having five leaflets, and in ranging from coast to coast and from Winnipeg to Mexico. The leaves of eastern forms are largest and bright glossy green.*

 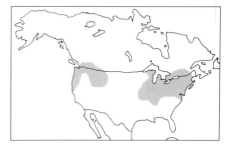

Horse Chestnut *This large-growing, coarse buckeye has been much planted in streets. The flowers are on 1ft panicles and open with chrome yellow blotches which turn crimson when the flower has been pollinated. The fruit husks have spines.*

 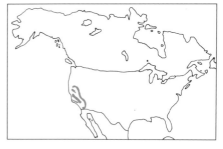

California Buckeye *A low tree of the foothills, this has small leaves with well-stalked leaflets. In summer they turn brown and nearly black, then fall early. The smooth pear-shaped fruits project on curved stalks.*

 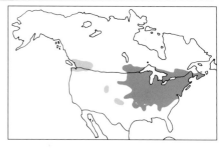

American Basswood *Distinguished from other lindens by the shiny rich green leaves with prominent systems of parallel veins. This makes a shapely tree in city streets. It is a frequent victim of sapsuckers.*

 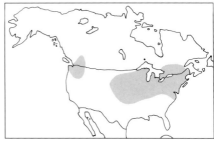

Small-leaf Linden *An attractive north European species which has been found to be well adapted to cities as far south as DC. The flowers are small and bright yellow in spreading sprays, not hanging as in most other lindens.*

Black Tupelo *This tree resembles Sourwood, in the craggy bark and elliptic leaves but it has smooth leaf margins. Fall colors progress from pale yellow to mottled yellow, orange and red until fully bright red.*

 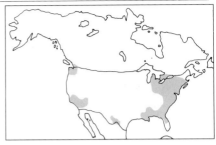

Golden Raintree *The flowers are bright yellow but small and sparsely set on an open 15in panicle, so they are less prominent than the pink bladder-like fruits. From SC south, the Formosan species bears big bunches of fruit and flowers.*

Bluegum Eucalyptus *A rampant fast-growing tree which flowers and fruits all the year in CA, spreading seedlings which grow 6ft a year. It is the only common gum with solitary, large fruits, bloomed bright blue-white.*

 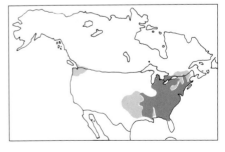

Flowering Dogwood *A small tree seldom more than 3½ft in girth, but prominent in winter with checkered red-brown bark and with shoots tipped by flower-buds. Spectacular in flower, also in fall with dark red foliage and red berries.*

 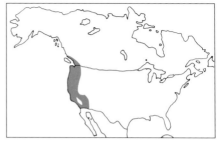

Pacific Dogwood *A taller tree than the Flowering Dogwood, with smooth bark and six un-notched bracts surrounding the flowerheads instead of four with notched tips. It opens a second set of flowers among the red leaves during the fall.*

 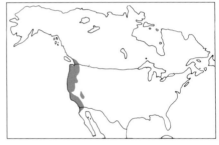

Pacific Madrone *An evergreen with dark orange-red branches and big smooth patches of pink on the trunk. It grows from Vancouver Island along the western slopes to the Mexican border. Erect plumes of white flowers open in late spring.*

Sourwood *Little urn-shaped white flowers grow in long, curved sprays and mature into capsules of similar size and color as the leaves turn bright red in the fall. The slender elliptic leaves are finely toothed.*

Common Persimmon *The 1½in fruits are much smaller than the Chinese persimmons in the shops, but they are prized as food after frosting. In late summer they hang, pale orange among the blackish leaves. The dark brown bark is in small plates.*

 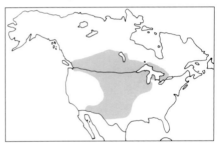

Russian Olive *This is no relation of the Olive, belonging to a different family. A tough, large shrub from western Asia, it is silvery gray and much planted for shelter in the prairie regions.*

White Ash *The biggest ash outside Mexico and the most distinct in fall colors. From yellow, the leaves turn orange and then purplish. Male and female flowers are on different trees. The undersides of the leaves are whitish green.*

Oregon Ash *The only ash of the Pacific slopes, this tree just fails to extend into Canada, but is sometimes planted there. Dense, soft, pale hairs cover the leaf undersides and shoots. Male and female flowers are on separate trees.*

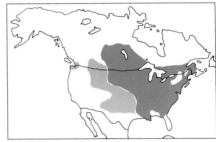

Green Ash *This includes the form often separated as Red Ash and is highly variable in the presence of dense, soft hairs. The Green form has stout shoots, quite smooth and shining bright green. Fall colors are bright yellow.*

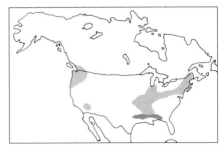

Southern Catalpa *Native to near the Gulf Coast, this tree has long been planted northward to provide durable fencepost timber and is now a park, garden and street tree from ON to WA. The 15in long capsules resemble bean-pods.*

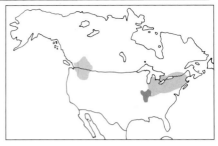

Northern Catalpa *Now as widespread as Southern Catalpa, this tree is distinguished by its ridged bark, taller and more upright crown, and longer, narrower leaf-tips. The foliage is yellower green and the fall color bright yellow.*

Peppertree *A native of Peru, this tree has taken over huge areas of Mexico and is a common street tree in southwest CA. The long, pinnate leaves hang in plumes and the dark red fruits hang in long bunches among them in summer.*

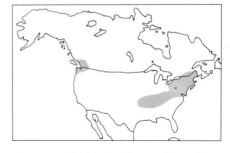

Royal Paulownia *A tree of very rapid, often fragile growth, reaching a good size but no great age. The heads of brown hairy flower buds tip each shoot through the winter and open in late spring if not damaged by frost.*

 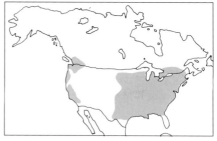

Ginkgo *Once distributed worldwide, this relict species only survived in China. The first two in N. America, planted in 1784 at Woodlands Cemetery, Philadelphia, were destroyed by lightning in 1985. It is now found in almost every city.*

 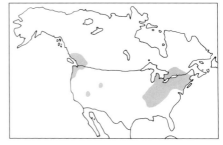

English Yew *A very slow-growing tree, which can live for some 3000 years in England, but has not reached great size in N. America. It has exceedingly strong timber and is unequalled for clipping into various shapes.*

Monkey-puzzle *A primitive tree from the Andes on the Chile-Argentine border and seen frequently only in the Puget Sound area. Male trees bear large catkins at branch-tips and females grow big globular cones taking three years to ripen.*

Bunya-Bunya Pine *Coming from Queensland, Australia, this tree can survive only a slight frost and needs hot summers. It has hanging, yellowish green shoots and deeply wrinkled bark.*

Norfolk Island Pine *The peculiar crown is typical of sub-tropical towns everywhere. Young trees have bright green spreading leaves incurved at the tips. On older trees the leaves are dull yellow-green and pressed to the shoots.*

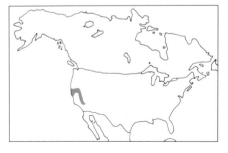

California Torreya *This native of the humid, low hill-country has hard, rather stiff, spine-tipped 3in leaves. Male flowers form globules beneath each leaf; plum-like fruits, on separate trees, are green turning purple.*

 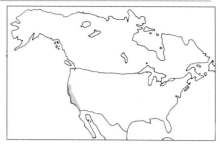

Monterey Cypress *In the tiny native stand at Point Lobos, old trees are squat and wide-spreading. Young trees there and planted nearby are bizarre, with wandering rope-like branches. Further north old trees are columnar.*

Eastern Redcedar *This juniper spreads rapidly onto unused ground and varies in color of foliage from very dark green to pale blue-green. The fruits, produced on separate trees from the male flowers, add to the blue-white appearance.*

 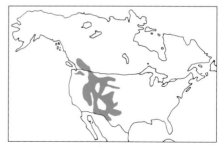

Rocky Mountain Juniper *This differs from Eastern Redcedar only in male flowers having more stamens and fruits taking two years to ripen. Their natural ranges are well separated, but planted trees can be difficult to distinguish.*

Western Redcedar *A cypress relative which can be 200ft tall and over 30ft round the trunk. The foliage readily emits a scent of apples or acetone. Planted sometimes in the east, it makes a neat, conic, bright green tree.*

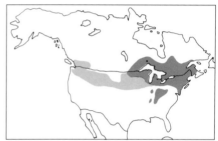

Northern White Cedar *This is a much smaller, shorter-lived tree of wet, east coast woods. The leaves are matt yellow-green beneath and have the scent of apple-peel. The pale brown bark comes away in thin, often spiralled strips.*

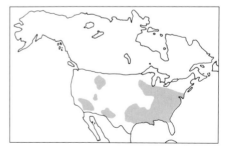

Oriental Arbor-vitae *Equally at home in humid or near-desert heat, this upright, dense ovoid tree is often planted each side of the front path. The foliage is bright green on both sides and its many gray-blue cones have curved backs.*

 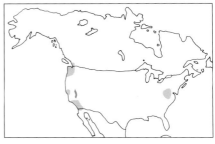

Giant Sequoia *Also known as 'Sierra Redwood' to distinguish it from the 'Coast Redwood', this tree may live 4000 years. 'General Sherman' has the biggest timber volume of any tree known. Trees from MA to DC grow low and branchy.*

Redwood *Many of the trees in the Redwood groves are 340–350ft tall, the tallest forest stands in the world. Highway 101 has 49 miles unbroken in the Avenue of The Giants. In old stands the bark is often pale gray.*

Baldcypress *This deciduous redwood sheds its shoots with the little leaves they bear, and leafs out bright fresh green late in the spring. It has been widely planted outside its native east coast and Mississippi bottomlands.*

Noble Fir *This silver fir stands out in the forests of the Cascades and some high Coast Range mountains because of its variably blue-gray foliage. A selected blue form, 'Glauca' is grown, but rarely thrives in eastern gardens.*

 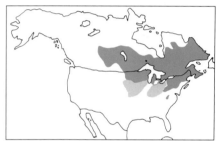

Balsam Fir *The common silver fir of the northeastern hills and bogs across to Alberta, spreading widely out of woods on to roadside banks and fields. The leaves have two broad silver bands beneath and a silver splash above near the tip.*

 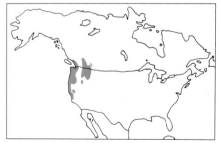

Grand Fir *Large pure stands grow on the eastern flanks of the Cascades but the trees are not as big as in the scattered remnants near the coast, where trees to 250ft high or more are occasional.*

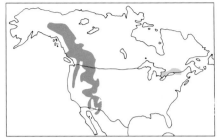

Subalpine Fir *This tree forms very slender snow-shedding spires at 5000 – 7000ft in BC and the Cascades and at 10,000ft in southern passes. In the Olympic Mountains, very broad skirts spread from their bases and remain under the snow.*

Douglas Fir *Related more to spruces and hemlocks than to silver firs, this tree has slender, pointed buds and soft, fruity scented foliage. Three-pronged bracts protrude from the cones. Trees over 250ft tall are seen in many groves.*

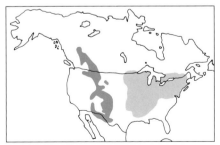

Rocky Mountain Douglas Fir *The central and eastern Rockies form of Douglas Fir, and often planted in the east. It has blackish bark, often bluer foliage and the three-pronged bracts on the cones extend further and curve downwards.*

 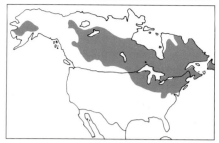

Tamarack *A tree of the muskeg in the north and northeastern hills. It opens tiny bright, deep red flowers before the leaves unfold. They ripen into a few small, few-scaled cones. The purple-brown bark is unridged, smooth but scaly.*

 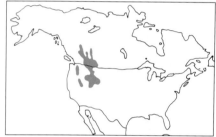

Western Larch *The biggest of the world's ten larches, this tree can be 200ft tall, but it adapts poorly to being grown out of range. Plantation larches in the east are of European or Japanese Larch.*

 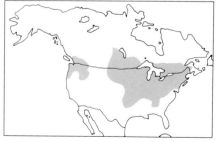

Norway Spruce *This European tree is amongst the commonest trees seen, from PA to New England and ON. Two forms occur at random, the 'comb' with shoots hanging in rows from level branches and the 'brush' with normal dense crowns.*

 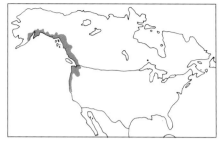

Sitka Spruce *From Kodiak Island to Mendocino, CA this tree grows almost everywhere within sight of tidal water. Vast trees once grew in BC and WA but only a few remain, by the Hoh River, WA. Windswept stands crown the cliffs of OR.*

 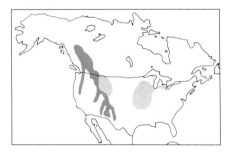

Engelmann Spruce *Resembles Blue Spruce but has soft, menthol-scented darker foliage, more slender shoots and orange-brown flaking bark. The cones are cylindrical, 2in long, curved and purplish brown.*

 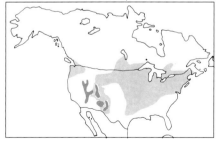

Blue Spruce *Native to the high ranges of WY and CO, this is one of the commonest town and garden trees from MB to TX and ME, and around Puget Sound, in many selected blue-white forms. It has broad cones with hard, crinkled white scales.*

 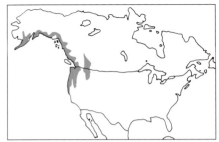

Western Hemlock *The finest of all hemlocks; an elegant tree to over 230ft with pendulous fine foliage. The leaves are of mixed sizes on the hairy shoots and have broad silvery bands beneath. It seems unable to grow in the east.*

Eastern Hemlock *The common hemlock of the northeast and abundant throughout its range and planted a little beyond. Around PA and DC it is now badly infested with an aphid, and garden trees have to be sprayed to survive.*

 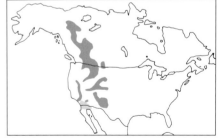

Lodgepole Pine *The pine of the Yellowstone NP geyser areas and the interior Rocky Mountains generally. The paired needles are leathery and flattened. The cones have small, sharp spines and are held closed on the tree until fire.*

Shore Pine *The form of the Lodgepole Pine from the sea to the Coast Ranges, with more densely held, thinner needles and bark broken into square blocks. Young trees grow 3ft shoots until the ocean winds affect them.*

 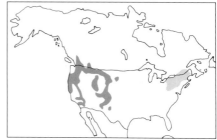

Ponderosa Pine *This tree has 10in needles in threes spraying out from stout shoots, a fine straight trunk with brown to bright orange flaking bark, and a neat conic crown of great height. It is one of the great trees of the world.*

Knobcone Pine *The long-conic cones of this pine have protruding spines and are held in long, dense clusters close around the upper stem and main branches. The crown is upswept with bright grassy-green foliage.*

Shortleaf Pine *This tree has sprouts on its trunk like the Pitch Pine, but it has a much more open crown, with drooping branches showing masses of retained 2in ovoid cones. It has needles in twos and threes.*

Slash Pine *This southern tree has its needles in twos and threes; they are 10–12in long and lemon-scented when broken. The shoots are stout, ridged and bloomed violet on pale red-brown. The dull purple-gray bark is coarsely short-ridged.*

Pitch Pine *A broadly domed tree with few large branches, which are, like the trunk, nearly covered in masses of hanging, slender, bright green sprouts. The bark is brown, deeply fissured into big ridges.*

 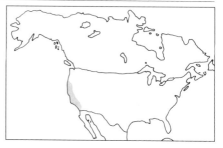

Monterey Pine *A three-needle pine with heavy ovoid cones. In the small native area it is attacked by mistletoe and dies young. Narrow young trees are seen planted by the coast to the north and south.*

Pinyon Pine *The pine of the Grand Canyon, AZ, and of large areas in the mountains of that region and southwards. The large edible seeds are borne in broad, flattened cones with few, thick scales.*

Singleleaf Pinyon Pine *This curious little tree makes upswept conic bushes of pale gray-green foliage, slightly blued by high passes or on the southwestern plateaux. Each needle is solitary, round in cross section and spine-tipped.*

Loblolly Pine *This is the major timber tree in the south-east and stands of trees with long clear trunks are common from SC to TX. The 5in cones are long-conic with short spines on the scales. The slender 6in needles are in threes.*

Sugar Pine *The tallest pine in the world, with Ponderosa, and many trees over 220ft tall survive in the Siskiyou and Yosemite areas. Long level branches stretch out from 150ft up the stem and are tipped by hanging cones up to 2ft long.*

 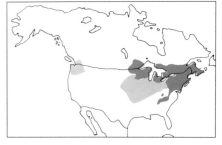

Eastern White Pine *The common five-needle pine of the northeast. Needles are rarely held for more than two years, so it has an airy open crown. Known before logging to grow over 200ft tall, few are now left over 130ft.*

California Washingtonia *A stout-stemmed palm, unlike the slender-stemmed Mexican Washingtonia which resembles a feather duster and grows all round Los Angeles. Both species hold a mat of dead leaves pressed to their upper stems.*

Canary Palm *The noblest of palms with arching 20ft bright green leaves and 5ft orange-stemmed flowerheads. It makes the Date Palm look dumpy, dowdy and spiky. Palms do not branch and their trunks have no annual rings.*

 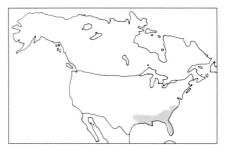

Cabbage Palmetto *Interlaced leaf-bases on the stem are often cleaned off in streets. The round leaves are about 10ft across, deeply cut into slender lobes; their stalks are 6ft long, rounded slightly above and deeply keeled.*

Index

Illustrations are indicated by
page numbers shown in bold
type.

H

Hackberry/Nettletree
(*Celtis*) 50–1
 Common (*C.
  occidentalis*) 50, **51**
 Netleaf (*C. reticulata*) 51
 Sugarberry (*C. laevigata*) 50
  51
Hawthorn (*Crataegus*) 62–3
 Black (*C. douglasii*) 62, **63**
 Cockspur (*C. crus-galli*) 62,
  63
 Downy (*C. mollis*) 62, **63**
 One-seed (*C.
  monogyna*) 62–3
 Paul's Scarlet (*C. oxycantha
  'Paul's Scarlet'*) 63
 Washington (*C.
  phaenopyrum*) 62
Hemlock (*Tsuga*) 103, 146–7
 Eastern (*T.
  canadensis*) 146–7
 Mountain (*T.
  mertensiana*) **146**, 147
 Western (*T.
  heterophylla*) 146, **147**
Hickory (*Carya*) 22–3
 Bitternut (*C. cordiformis*) 22
 Mockernut (*C.
  tomentosa*) 23
 Pecan (*C. illinoensis*) 22, **23**
 Shagbark (*C. ovata*) 22–3
Holly (*Ilex*) 82–3
 American (*I. opaca*) 82
 Dahoon (*I. cassine*) 82, **83**
 European (*I.
  aquifolium*) 82–3
  'Golden Milkmaid' 83
  Hedgehog 'Ferox' 83
  Perry's Weeping
   ('Albomarginata') 83
  Weeping ('Pendula') 83
  Yellow-berried
   ('Bacciflava') 83
 Yaupon (*I. vomitoria*) 82, **83**
Honeylocust (*Gleditsia
  macanthos*) 80, **81**
Hophornbeam (*Ostrya*) 30, 31

Eastern (*O. virginiana*) **30**,
  31
Hornbeam (*Carpinus*) 30–1
 American (Blue/Water Beech,
  Ironwood) (*C.
  caroliniana*) 30, **31**
 European (*C. betulus*) 30–1
  Pyramidal 'Fastigiata' 30
Horse Chestnut (*Aesculus
  hippocastanum*) 90–1
 American *see* Buckeye
  (American Horse
  Chestnut)
 Red (*Aesculus × carnea*) **90**,
  91

I

Ilex see Holly (*Ilex*)

J

Joshua Tree (*Yucca
  brevifolia*) 110
Juglans see Walnut (*Juglans*)
Juniper (*Juniperus*) 122–3
 Common (*J. communis*) 122
  Dwarf (var. *nana*) **122**
 Eastern Redcedar (*J.
  virginiana*) 122, **123**
 Rocky Mountain (*J.
  scopulorum*) 122, **123**
 Utah (*J. osteosperma*) 122,
  123
 Western/Sierra (*J.
  occidentalis*) 122, **123**
Juniperus 122–3

K

Keaki (*Zelkova serrata*) **50**, 51
Kentucky Coffee-tree
  (*Gymnocladus dioicus*) 80

L

Laburnum see Golden Chain
  Tree, Voss's

O

P

NOTES